Insider Internet Marketing

By JDD Publishing

Insider Internet Marketing
by JDD Publishing

Written and Published by Jim Daniels
Email JDD@JDD-Publishing.com

Edited by Laura E. Kelly
Professional Editing Services: Email
Editor@JDD-Publishing.com

ISBN 0-9659037-0-2

http://www.bizweb2000.com

As the internet rapidly evolves, this book will evolve with it. Although all contact information is checked prior to each print run, if you experience any problems with email or web addresses in this book, email Updates@JDD-Publishing.com for a free email update.

INTRODUCTION

PHASE 1 :

POWERFUL E-MARKETING

PHASE 2 :

WORKING THE WEB

INTRODUCTION

ALL FACTS - NO THEORY

Before you embark on your journey through this publication, I'd like to make one thing perfectly clear. The information you are about to discover is *not* textbook stuff. You won't stumble upon much, if any, of this stuff in your college studies.

Every bit of knowledge found between the covers of this book consists of nothing but cold hard cybermarketing facts. That's right, not "real world knowledge," but information directly from cyberspace.

Real world marketing and cyberspace marketing are two separate environments. Oh, you'll find plenty of similarities, but there is one fact that will not go away...

Entrepreneurship in Cyberspace is for *everyone.*

If you're fortunate enough to own a computer with a modem, you can make money in this new frontier. Unlike the real world, you do *not* need a large marketing budget to make money on the internet.

This publication will teach you *all* of the inside strategies *that work.*

I've made it my mission to leave out all *theories* about internet marketing in this publication. Theories don't usually end up making you much money. That is unless your name is Einstein. I present to you only *facts.* Facts based on a proven, successful internet marketing campaign. This is the stuff I have utilized to build a thriving internet-based business from ground zero.

There was a time when I was new to this medium. From day one I scratched and clawed for information to help my business succeed. I spent hours upon hours of time surfing the World Wide Web for inside secrets. What I couldn't get for free, I paid for. I did whatever it took to learn as much as I could about this new marketing arena. Every time I learned a new trick or strategy, I tested it inside and out.

This endless quest for information has resulted in a thriving internet-based business.

I know firsthand what it takes to make money online and I'm about to teach you everything I know.

So when you get done reading this publication, do yourself a favor and read it again. Make notes when you come across an idea you can use in your own business model. Take out your yellow marker and highlight key resources (**in bold**) and tips you wish to employ. Try the tips and strategies that have brought me so much success. They work or they wouldn't be in here.

There's real money to be made in cyberspace. I invite you to go and get your share!

CYBERSPACE GOLD RUSH?

Is it really possible to make enough money on the internet to quit your day job? I'd like to briefly share my own experience with you so that you can learn firsthand that not only is it possible, it's not even that difficult!

Actually, my success story is becoming an increasingly familiar account of "blue collar worker turned netrepreneur." After working for 10 years as a technician and service manager for a small telecommunications company in Boston, Mass., I managed to shed my day job and go to work in cyberspace. Unlike the growing number of others who have accomplished this feat, my story is unique in that I started with almost zero capital and a very limited understanding of the internet. I actually trained myself on the net then put the training into action. Now I enjoy the benefits of owning my own home-based business with a continually growing income.

Here's how it all happened. In February 1996, I decided to check out all the hoopla I had been hearing about this internet thing. With my modest tax return, I purchased a used 386 computer and a modem. Little did I know at the time that this investment of just more than $300 would blossom into a new career within a year.

Since I had a pretty fair working knowledge of computers, getting online wasn't too difficult. One night after work I stuck that free America Online (AOL) disk in my floppy drive and followed the instructions. Once connected, I started doing some research. Realizing that I was just one of a few million people with the same dream of making money in cyberspace, I knew I would need to learn as much about this new medium as possible. After all, my dream was to someday make enough money to render my day job unnecessary.

So out I went, onto the World Wide Web, to weed through all of the newest methods of online marketing. After three months of research I developed a plan. I figured that if I could offer some solid guidance to the growing army of wannabe netrepreneurs, I might make some money in the process. I took the results of my research and condensed it into a 40-page manual. The manual was designed to save everyone else the endless hours of research I had just been through. After all, if someone had offered all the answers to me back when I was a "newbie," I would certainly have spent a few bucks to get a jump out of the gate. I titled the manual "Internet Email! Beyond The Basics!"

With my self-published manual and new found wisdom of the ins and outs of internet marketing, I formed JDD Publishing Co. and set out to market my publication online. As it turns out, my idea was right on target. There **was** a huge demand for information about starting a low cost, effective online marketing campaign. Within the first few months I managed to peddle more than 500 copies of my new publication. Just the confidence builder I needed!

Just eight months after I started, I sat down and figured out that my still-growing income from this part-time venture had surpassed my weekly paycheck from my full-time job. "Someday" had come a lot sooner than I expected. The next time I sat at my computer it was to compose my resignation letter!

Since then my opportunities have multiplied at a rate I never dreamed of. I started publishing a free email newsletter "The BizWeb E-Gazette," which I currently email every Friday to my growing list of 15,000 subscribers. The newsletter features online marketing tips, articles and low-cost business classified advertising.

From there I migrated my business from the shoestring budget email marketing to the World Wide Web. The knowledge I gained from that migration experience is revealed in this, the newest of my publications. With the way things are expanding on the internet, the future certainly looks bright for JDD Publishing and it can look bright for your business!

So there you have it. Living proof that it is possible to make a living in cyberspace. That's right, you don't need a big bankroll. You don't need to be a "techie." And best of all, you can start today by working part-time in the comfort of your own home!

HOW A LOW BUDGET COMPANY COMPETES AGAINST THE BIG PLAYERS

So you're considering establishing a business in the online arena. Good thinking. Hopefully you're doing it for the right reasons and not just because you've heard that *all* businesses will be on the net sooner or later.

Consider the following as proof that you've made the right decision.

The mid-1990s has seen the population on "the net" increase to numbers previously unthought of. This unprecedented growth has opened up a whole new playing field for upstart entrepreneurs. The time is certainly ripe for newcomers to take charge and that's exactly what's happening!

Given the technological advances in today's society, home-based businesses themselves can do nothing but get stronger and stronger. With personal computers now in one out of every four homes across America, it will soon be unnecessary to leave the home for anything at all. After all, one would already be hard pressed to think of a single item that is not readily available via the internet.

There is no question that the internet itself is developing into the most powerful marketing medium since television. From an entrepreneur's standpoint, this new online era is leveling the playing field forever by providing cheaper and more effective marketing tools.

If you're like most marketers, you're probably getting

around to asking the big question everyone else seems to be asking: "Is anyone really buying anything online?"

Absolutely! But just who are the customers in cyberspace? Well believe it or not, most of them haven't even arrived yet! That's right, it's not too late for you to set up shop. Many industry experts expect more than 100 million people to be connected by the turn of the century. Your potential customer base is virtually unlimited. Needless to say, with the right product or service, strategically marketed to the right consumer, a company can make quite a profit.

Keep in mind however, that some products and services are great for the net while others are not. Here's a good rule of thumb in determining if online marketing would work for you. If you have a product or service that could serve a national or global marketplace effectively, you can use the internet to market it. Remember, you must also be able to deliver the goods.

JDD Publishing found that fact out quickly when orders were received from places like Malaysia, Portugal, Switzerland, and Singapore. Within months, customers in more than 30 countries were served, proving that this truly is an international marketplace.

If you have an idea for a product or service that may prove profitable on the internet, you've come to the right place. This book will teach you not only how to profit online, but how to prosper!

EMAIL - THE GREAT EQUALIZER

Although there are many reasons why the internet is breeding a large number of successful new entrepreneurs, you must be aware of the one tool in particular that has been largely responsible - EMAIL.

In the introduction I wrote that online marketing is for everyone. So what is it exactly that proves to be the "equalizer?" Cheaper and more effective tools, namely email. The high costs associated with running a business are gone forever. The ability to utilize inexpensive business tools such as email, is the golden key to your success.

Email is without a doubt, the most powerful marketing tool born from the internet. Many predicted the World Wide Web would be the biggest marketing advantage the internet provides. Although a great web site can be an extremely effective tool for online marketing (as you'll see later in this book) without email the web would be far less effective for business. From an entrepreneurial standpoint, internet email is the glue that holds every online marketing aspect together. Moreover, it accomplishes this feat seamlessly and tirelessly.

Can you think of any other way to reach someone on the other side of the globe in seconds, 24 hours a day? All the while doing it for pennies? Not a chance! Nothing in marketing has ever come close to the power of email.

In this book you will learn to harness the incredible power of email, as you explore the world of direct email, autoresponders (auto-reply email) and the most powerful list of ezines (email newsletters) ever composed.

Always remember this: **Email is the single most effective business tool ever invented.** Don't make the mistake of getting away from email marketing. Even as you discover other powerful online marketing strategies, email will remain number one.

A MODEL OF SUCCESS

As I stated at the start of this book, the information found in this publication is based on fact alone. The fact is, JDD Publishing has used each and every tip and strategy described in this book to become one of the leaders in providing information to online marketers across the globe.

My business model can be closely replicated by absolutely anyone with the same strong urge to succeed.

I will not go into your choice of product or service that you will be marketing. I realize there are millions of different products and services being marketed in the world. Keep in mind however, that some products and services are great for the net while others are not.

As I stated earlier: If you have a product or service that could serve a national or global marketplace effectively, you can use the internet to market it.

Assuming your product or service is sound, the basic principles outlined here can be applied to nearly any online business venture. Naturally, the size of your budget will invariably alter the exact steps you take. For instance, you may decide to hire someone to design your web pages instead of taking on the task yourself. The point I'm trying to make is this. No matter what your budget is, there are certain steps you *must* take online to give yourself the best chance to succeed.

The following is a rough model of our successful

online marketing campaign. As you can see, there are basically two phases to a successful campaign. Each phase contains some simple steps to follow and are explained in detail in future chapters.

PHASE 1
Start With Simple Low Cost Email Marketing.

a. Set up autoresponders for *all* products/services.
b. Utilize free/low cost classified advertising.
c. Market in newsgroups.
d. Market in discussion groups.
e. Consider direct email vs. bulk email.
f. Utilize ezine advertising. (Use our power list!)

PHASE 2
Work The World Wide Web.

a. Find someone to build your site or do it yourself.
b. Design a "marketing friendly" site.
c. Register your domain.
d. Find a host and set up shop.
e. Promote your site online.
f. Promote your site offline.
g. Build traffic with our inside strategies.

There. That's it. Looks simple doesn't it. Actually it is simple. As long as you use as much of the information you learn in this book as possible, your success is imminent. Go forth. Read. Re-read. And take action.

PHASE ONE:

POWERFUL E-MARKETING

ISN'T IT ALL ABOUT THE WEB?

Now that you know it's feasible for absolutely anyone with a computer to become their own boss, let's take a look at exactly how to get the ball rolling once you're online. After all, *saying* it can be done on a limited budget is one thing, actually *doing* it is another.

As the previous outline explained, an effective internet marketing campaign can be broken down into two distinct parts. Although the two parts ultimately work together to accomplish the same goals, it's important to be aware of the difference.

First, there is what I like to call **e-marketing**. E-marketing can take on many forms as you'll see in this chapter. Which of the different forms of e-marketing an individual chooses to employ is strictly a matter of style or choice. Some prefer the hard hitting tactics of direct bulk email, while others, like myself, rely heavily on milder forms of "direct" email like ezine advertising to bring in qualified leads. More on these tactics in a minute.

The second distinct part of internet marketing is what you'll learn in phase two, **web marketing**. Web marketing can be a very effective part of your internet marketing campaign. But, it can also be very expensive. We'll teach you how to cut all the costs you can, but more on that later.

Let's delve into e-marketing. The following sections will break down the e-marketing part of your campaign by introducing you to some low-cost methods of getting leads. Unless you are brand new to this medium, you are probably aware of some of these methods. It's important to follow along anyway as you'll pick up many new and valuable resources.

A MUST: THE AUTORESPONDER

One component that I consider an absolute *must*, no matter how small (or large) your online marketing budget, is called the *autoresponder*. Even if you're familiar with autoresponders I urge you to read this section, because you may be paying too much for your autoresponders.

An autoresponder allows you to have your sales letter (or any other email message) delivered 24 hours a day and within seconds of receiving a request. And believe it or not, you can purchase autoresponders for less than $3 per month! (See the end of this section.)

Anyone who's using the internet to market their products or services should use autoresponders. I currently have 12 in action and will be going beyond 20 by the end of 1997. Also known as a "mailbot" or "infobot", there are numerous companies that provide this service on the net.

Here's how it works. Upon reading one of your web pages or advertisements, a prospective customer decides to reply and get "more information." The email address they are instructed to reply to is not your own, but the address of your autoresponder. As soon as any message is received by the autoresponder, it automatically sends out your "more information" or sales letter. (Usually within seconds!)

There are a few things to be aware of before getting an autoresponder. First of all, be sure to go with a company that will give you an unlimited number of "hits" or autoresponses. The last thing you want is to pay a "per response" rate when you start getting a lot of replies.

Also be sure that you'll get a copy of each inquiry, so you'll be able to track your marketing efforts. (Always tell prospects to enter something in the subject box when requesting information. This will allow you to know exactly where they came from.)

Setting up an autoresponder is a piece of cake. Here's an example of how I set up new autoresponders with InfoBack Corp., in my opinion the best autoresponder company on the internet.

Once I decide on an address (such as infofree@infoback.net) I check to make sure the address is not currently in use. Next I compose an email message that contains my sales letter for this particular autoresponder. Then I simply send the email message to my new address (infofree@infoback.net) with my password in the subject line. That's it, my new autoresponder is now active. I repeat this same procedure each time I want to make a change to my message. (They don't charge for changes, but be careful, some companies do.)

Note how simple the above procedure was. This is one of the many reasons I decided to go with InfoBack. Other companies require you to make changes to your autoresponders on the World Wide Web, which can be a hassle depending on the type of browser you use. Below is a great example of why you need to be able to make changes quickly and easily. If you're a subscriber to my

BizWeb E-Gazette you may have read the following in my Tip of the Week section in the Feb 14, 1997 issue:

This weeks tip... "Plan B"

This week's tip is a little different than most. It stems from a personal business experience which occurred just last weekend.

As many of you know, all addresses at our JDD-Publishing.com domain were undeliverable over the weekend of Friday, Feb. 7 until Monday, Feb. 10. This was the result of a problem at the company where I registered this domain. (We'll be moving it from their servers- but that's another story!)

The tip I'd like to present today is based on this trying experience. Being a relatively small internet-based business that does 90% of our correspondence via email, the effects of this down time could have resulted in a ton of lost business.

Since many of our customers are also small and home based businesses, many of our inquiries and orders come on weekends.

After a little scrambling, I whipped up a plan B which enabled us to receive correspondence throughout the ordeal. Take a quick look through the steps I took. Perhaps you can use them to prepare for your own unexpected roadblock. Upon learning of the problem (Saturday AM) I immediately took the following steps.

Step 1.

Most of our advertising listed our autoresponder addresses, so everyone was still receiving our sales information. I simply changed the contact address listed in each of those AR sales letters. Since all of our autoresponders offer a "quick change" feature this was a breeze.

Step 2.

I notified all of our recent inquiries (which are all saved to a folder in our Eudora email program) of our secondary email address. Many online marketers carry a secondary account for this very reason. Twenty dollars per month is an inexpensive insurance policy, plus it offers a second gateway to the internet for those days you have trouble logging on through your main carrier.)

Step 3.

I changed all of the email addresses listed in our Web Pages to the secondary address and uploaded the changes to our server. (Yet another reason to maintain your own web site.)

Step 4.

Tried desperately to forget about the whole thing until Monday.

When I fired up the ol' computer Monday morning, although our main email address was still inoperable, I had the usual number of inquiries and orders waiting to be processed. Our Plan B had succeeded.

Moral of the story? Don't count on others to bail you out in time of crisis. Be prepared to take action and prevent further damage yourself. Always have a Plan B!

As you can see, autoresponders not only provide you with a means to get your sales information (or any other information you wish to offer) to your prospects and customers, they provide a nice little safety net when used properly.

Take heed of this one important note about autoresponders: **If you plan on doing any unsolicited emailing don't use your autoresponder address in the mailing.** Your autoresponder will be subject to cancellation upon the first sign of spamming (sending unsolicited bulk email). It won't take long for them to see some flaming (harsh replies) or email bombing (repeated flames). It is unfair to subject the autoresponder's server to such attacks.

TIP: Consider using InfoBack Corp's autoresponder services called "email on demand." Visit **http://www.bizweb2000.com/arsonly.htm** for details. * As of 1997, InfoBack's autoresponder prices were as low as $29.95 per month for 10 autoresponders. That's less than $3 each!

If you prefer to have your autoresponder addresses in *your own* domain name, here's an excellent resource: **http://www.bizweb2000.com/virtual.htm**

At that URL you will find a special report on web hosting. Follow the link to the company called Virtualis. This is where I host my web site. Their MEGA web hosting option is one of the best hosting deals on the internet. It comes with tons of innovative features and an unlimited supply of autoresponders. This one-stop web services option will give you every single internet marketing service you'll ever need, all under one simple plan. In addition, you can earn a healthy income by referring others!

A LIMITED BUDGET TECHNIQUE: FREE AND LOW-COST CLASSIFIEDS

Okay. On with some e-marketing methods.

The first method you should consider, especially if your budget is limited, are free and low-cost classified ads that you post yourself. These breakdown into two separate areas. There are the "Major Provider" classifieds found on AOL and Compuserve, and there are the World Wide Web classifieds found on the web.

Major Provider Classifieds

AOL and Compuserve classifieds are very popular and inexpensive to post. You simply post your ad and instruct interested parties to inquire via email. Once they inquire, you send them details of your offer by return email.

But does posting classifieds in these sections really work? Sure it does. That's why you see the ad sections fill up so quickly. Don't expect to be bombarded with inquiries, however, if you regularly post ads in these sites, you will receive some action. The key is to regularly post.

AOL users: To get to the AOL classified section, from the main menu, click on "Marketplace". Next click on "classifieds & advertising". From the next screen you can choose between placing a "premier ad" (paid advertisement) or going to the "Bulletin Boards" and placing a free ad. Make sure you find the group that will most target your prospective customers.

Also, be sure to use a catchy headline or subject. This is what people will see when browsing through the ads, so enter something that will catch their eye. After posting, if you want to see your ad, you must exit that section and come back to it.

Note: Because there are so many people using AOL classified advertising, your ad will only last a short time (especially free ads at the bulletin boards). You must replace them frequently.

AOL limits bulletin board ad categories to 500 ads. To have your ad appear close to the top of the listing, watch the particular categories that are most appropriate for your ads and make a note of the time of day they reach the limit. If you post your ad as close to the deadline as possible, your ad is more likely to appear near the top. More people will see the ad this way.

Compuserve users: Here's how to place an ad on Compuserve. From the main menu, click on the green traffic light at the top of the screen. A box will appear with "go" at the top of it. Next, type in "classifieds" click on "OK" then click "access classifieds." Next choose an area and click submit. Then click on a subject. Now enter your name and state and your subject line. Next choose how many weeks you want your ad to run. Type in your ad text and click post. It usually takes 24 hours for your ad to show up.

The cut-off time for posting ads on Compuserve is

4:30 a.m. eastern-standard time. The ads placed right after 4:30 a.m. have the best chance of being near the top. Of course, you know the importance of this. How many times have you read much further than the first 25 or so messages?

NOTE: When using both AOL and Compuserve classified advertising, be sure to post *from* an address in which you do not mind receiving unsolicited email. Once you advertise at these sites, *your own* email address will be harvested many times over and you'll receive plenty of unsolicited email.

World Wide Web Classifieds

In addition to the major service providers' online classifieds, there are now more than 1,000 sites on the World Wide Web that offer free and low cost classifieds. Do they work? Sure. It's a little time consuming to post to them all, but these ads do result in inquiries. Usually no really large numbers, but a few per day are possible.

Point your browser to the following URL (Uniform Resource Locator) for a jumping off point to more than 1,000 free and low cost classified sites on the web: **http://www.uran.net/imall/mother.html**

Once you get to a classified site that accepts posts related to what you have to offer, you post your classified ads in the appropriate section (business, hobbies, books etc.). Just like the classified sections of AOL and

Compuserve, anyone who reads your classified then requests more information by sending you email.

Once you receive the request, you simply email the prospective customer your sales literature. (Or better yet, they get it within seconds from your autoresponder.) They can then print the details (including an order form which should be on all your sales letters) and send their order.

NEWSGROUPS AND THE SIGNATURE

Newsgroups are forums where anyone can post messages similar to email about a specific topic (such as "internet marketing" or "advertising"). There are literally thousands of different newsgroups on the internet, covering just about any topic you can imagine.

Newsgroup marketing was very popular before the birth of the World Wide Web, though many online marketers still rely heavily on this strategy. Although not a huge fan of newsgroup marketing, I recently browsed some business-related newsgroups and checked out the traffic. What I saw was a steady flow of posts, some numbering above 100 per day. These raw numbers alone, lend support to the rationale that newsgroup marketing can be worthwhile.

Here's a fact that many internet "newbies" do not realize. Newsgroups are *not* intended for advertising. Although many newsgroups have developed into advertising forums, they were originally intended as areas to read and post messages for the purpose of assisting others interested in the same topic.

So how do you market your wares simply be posting messages that help others? Simple. You do it through a cleverly composed footer on each post called your "signature." To this day, this remains *the most effective* way to market through newsgroups.

Most email programs allow you to create a signature file to tell people a little about your business. If your program allows this, do it today. It's an excellent way to get some free advertising! Be sure to include your business name, your URL if you have one, the nature of your business and any contact information you wish to provide.

(A good sig file is between three and five lines long; no more than that.)

Once again, remember, some newsgroups allow you to post direct ads, while others expect this more tactful approach. For this reason, it is very important to get a feel for each newsgroup by lurking awhile and reading some other postings before posting your message.

With that said, here's a bit of a jump start. If you're interested in trying newsgroup marketing, the following list of business-related newsgroups should keep you busy a while:

alt.ad
alt.america.online
alt.bbs.ads
alt.bbs.internet
alt.biz.misc
alt.business
alt.business.accountability
alt.business.career-opportunities.executives
alt.business.home
alt.business.home.pc
alt.business.hospitality
alt.business.misc
alt.business.multi-level

alt.commerce.misc-ads
alt.internet.commerce
alt.internet.services
alt.make.money
alt.make.money.fast
aol.commerce.misc-ads
aol.commerce.mlm.announce
biz.comp.misc
biz.general
biz.marketplace
biz.misc
biz.mlm
biz.newgroup
biz.next.newprod
biz.univel.misc
can.atlantic.biz
market.internet.free
misc.business
misc.entrepreneurs

Although the world may not beat a path to your cyber-doorstep, newsgroup marketing is free. When used regularly, it can become an integral part of your online marketing campaign.

Note: A great web source for information on Usenet Newsgroups is Deja News at **http://dejanews.com/**. From there you can search and even post to newsgroups.

HARNESSING THE POWER OF BULK EMAIL AND DIRECT EMAIL

Caution: The title above mentions two distinctly different approaches to email marketing. DO NOT confuse the two.

Bulk Email

When I write "bulk email," I am referring to "unsolicited" bulk email - the practice of transmitting mass quantities of email to large lists of "unqualified" email addresses. This practice in itself is a controversial subject. You must be very careful when considering using bulk email to market your wares on the internet.

Unsolicited bulk email is NOT illegal. It is however frowned upon by many internet users.

You may have heard this practice of sending unsolicited bulk email referred to as "spamming." (Yes, the name comes from the famous comedy skit "Spam! Spam! Spam!" by Monty Python.) In the online world, spamming means sending unsolicited email directly to a list of ***unsuspecting*** email addresses or newsgroups.

It is common knowledge that you can actually purchase lists containing anywhere from a few thousand to over a million email addresses on the internet. Just go to your favorite search engine, such as www.infoseek.com and search on "bulk email". You'll find tons of people selling email addresses.

The simple fact is, unsolicited bulk email is considered

poor "netiquette" by many netizens. If you send unsolicited email to addresses that do not want commercial email, you can get into more trouble than you would expect.

Naturally the decision is yours, but if you're thinking of trying unsolicited bulk email, you must know two facts:

1. A large number of internet citizens DO NOT approve of unsolicited email and WILL complain to your Internet Service Provider (ISP).

2. Many ISP's will discontinue your account when they get complaints from angry recipients of your unsolicited bulk email.

Does sending your ad to thousands of unsuspecting addresses really work anyway? Do you really get any genuinely interested leads mixed in with all those flames? Well, although unsolicited bulk email probably isn't as effective as some people would like you to believe, it has received praise from many business owners.

Just why is bulk email so popular? Simple. It's far cheaper than traditional bulk mail. Traditional bulk mailing and bulk *email* advertising differ greatly in one major aspect - cost. The costs associated with traditional bulk mailing can cut deeply into potential profits immediately. Postage costs alone can break the bank. Bulk email does not have this downfall, although when not done properly, as I explained, it does come with its own set of pitfalls.

There are more and more sources of good qualified

email addresses becoming available online. If you have your heart set on trying a do-it-yourself bulk email marketing campaign, and don't mind fighting the few elements we've pointed out, there are still many intricacies to learn. I highly recommend you get your hands on a copy of "Internet Email! Beyond The Basics!" by yours truly. Among many other topics, it goes into detail on specific email programs and how to properly deliver large amounts of email with a minimum amount of time and effort. For more info on this publication, send email to our autoresponder address at infofree@infoback.net or visit our web page to learn more at **http://www.bizweb2000.com/prod02.htm**.

Direct Email

Now lets move on to a much more powerful and effective form of email marketing on the internet. It is more appropriately referred to as ***direct email advertising.***

I consider *direct* email to be the practice sending commercial email to a large number of recipients that **have approved** of commercial email. There are many companies on the internet offering such services and this can be a very effective internet marketing strategy.

If you really want to try bulk email marketing but aren't up to the rigors of unsolicited bulk email, consider hiring a company that specializes in direct email. One such company that manages commercial email lists on the internet is called Netcreations. Visit their site at **http://www.netcreations.com** for details.

Netcreations advertises a targeted email service which offers marketers a "politically correct" way to reach their target market on the net. As of early 1997, Netcreations had more than two million email addresses under management in more than 1,000 topical categories from aerobics to scuba diving. I've used their services and experienced excellent results. (More than 14 percent response factor and zero flames.) Although this targeted direct email marketing is more costly than unsolicited bulk email, it is far more effective.

Another alternative method of direct email advertising, which I rely on heavily at JDD Publishing is called ezine advertising. Ezine advertising is a growing internet marketing strategy because it offers a low cost way for advertisers to reach a very targeted audience. You'll learn all about ezine advertising in the next section.

EZINE ADVERTISING: THE BEST BANG FOR YOUR INTERNET ADVERTISING DOLLAR

An ezine, an online magazine or newsletter, is a rapidly expanding internet marketing tool. The number of ezines on the internet has exploded from a few hundred in 1994 to thousands in 1997. (It is growing too fast for an accurate count.) There are ezines on thousands of different subjects and many offer low-cost advertising.

Ezines are perhaps the most powerful and cost effective way to attract qualified prospects on the net. Inquiries numbering 25 to 50 or more can be received from a single inexpensive classified ad in a popular ezine.

Ezine advertising is a proven and growing online marketing medium. What makes ezine advertising work so well is that your ad is delivered directly to your target audience via email. It's simple for prospects to answer your ad, and best of all, they don't have to find your offer, your ad finds them!

Now before I go into details on ezine marketing, I must first explain the difference between the two distinct types of ezines on the net.

The first type of ezine is basically a web site. Anyone that has the web address can check out the ezine. Some are free and others charge a subscription fee. Although this type of ezine is very nice to look at (graphics and sometimes audio included) the marketing value is not nearly as strong as the next type.

The next type of ezine is delivered directly to your email address. The number of these ezines has begun to grow very rapidly, as more and more people jump on the internet. Most of these are free to subscribe to and run weekly. Although not as fancy (currently text only) this type of ezine is an excellent marketing tool.

Many of these email ezines are now offering paid advertising to online marketers. Not only do you reach your target audience, you reach them by the *thousands*. Of all the online marketing methods available, this could be the most effective.

Rates are generally determined by the number of subscribers that will see your ad. Some of the smaller ezines reach a few thousand subscribers and charge about $5 to $7 per line with a three line minimum. The larger ezines, with more than 100,000 subscribers usually get about $8 to $15 per line. (A line is usually 80 characters long.)

If you think these rates are high, compare them to traditional advertising rates found in major magazines. I think you'll agree that ezines offer a much better deal!

Another factor that makes ezine advertising great is how simple it is to respond to an ad. Interested parties simply send email for free details, or click to your web site, which takes them all of 10 seconds.

THE POWER EZINE LIST

The following list of ezines are what I call my "Power Ezine List." Simply put, this comprehensive list may very well end up playing a major role in *your* successful online marketing campaign.

If whatever you are marketing online doesn't fit into any of these business-related publications, fear not, there are ezines out there for you. This section will tell you how to find them.

Nearly all of the ezines on this list are delivered via email (a few good web "zines" are mixed in). Every ezine on the power list is chock full of helpful information for online marketers.

Furthermore, with the exception of just a few, the following ezines accept some form of advertising.

Put this list to work for your business!

Each ezine on the list contains the following 10 specifications for your review:

Publication Name
Editor/Publisher Name
Editor/Publisher Email Address
Cost Of Publication
Short Description
Type of Publication: (Email or Web)
Frequency of Publication
URL: (If appropriate)
Advertising Format
Subscribe Instructions

Now, on with the list...

"A Serious Business" - The International Small Business E-Letter
Editor/Publisher Name: Ray Gabriel editor/publisher
Email Address: editor@earthone.com
Cost of Publication: six months free trial/US$15.00 for 24 issues thereafter
Description: "International small business how-tos, resources, contacts and more from readers in more than 80 countries."
Type of Publication: Email newsletter
Frequency of Publication: Bi-weekly
URL: http://www.earthone.com
Advertising Format: None
Subscribe Instructions: For free trial send word "SUBSCRIBE" to Free@EarthOne.com or visit web site. Sample available from Sample@Earthone.com.

Abundant News
Editor/Publisher Name: Geoff Williams
Email Address: abundant@powerup.com.au
Cost of Publication: FREE
Description: Free email newsletter gives you tips on electronic marketing, profiting from the internet, home-based business, and news of big business on the net.
Type of Publication: Email newsletter
Frequency of Publication: Monthly
URL: http://www.powerup.com.au/~abundant/archive.htm
Advertising Format: Classified and Sponsorship.

Subscribe Instructions: Email abundant@powerup.com.au with "SUBSCRIBE Abundant News" in the subject line.

All About Money
Editor/Publisher Name: Sharon Tucci
Email Address: publisher@allaboutmoney.com
Cost of Publication: FREE
Description: A weekly ezine delivered via email dealing with Personal & Small Business Finance.
Type of Publication: Email newsletter
Frequency of Publication: Weekly
URL: N/A
Advertising Format: Free resource listing for people looking for work and companies with open positions along with a free business opportunity directory.
Subscribe Instructions: Send an email message to majordomo@po.databack.com with the words "subscribe allaboutmoney" in the message body.

The BizBot Weekly
Editor/Publisher Name: The BizBot Marketing Group.
Email Address: cfo@netten.net
Cost of Publication: FREE
Description: A free newsletter containing news, views, and how-to's from the exciting world of Internet Marketing. Great variety of classifieds.
Type of Publication: Email newsletter
Frequency of Publication: Weekly
URL: http://www.bizbotweekly.com
Advertising Format: Classifieds
Subscribe Instructions: Send email to the following

address: majordomo@angus.mystery.com - in the MESSAGE BODY put "subscribe bizbot" (without the quotes).

Bizhotline Online
Editor/Publisher Name: Frank Pines
Email Address: fpines@bizhotline.com
Cost of Publication: FREE
Description: Small and Home Based Business publication and an import/export wholesale product publication.
Type of Publication: Email newsletter
Frequency of Publication: Bi-weekly
URL: http://www.bizhotline.com
Advertising Format: Classifieds
Subscribe Instructions: Visit home page or email subscribe@bizhotline.com

Biz Tips Newsletter
Editor/Publisher Name: Wendy McClelland
Email Address: wendyweb@bizresource.com
Cost of Publication: FREE
Description: Biz tips, ideas, site reviews, book reviews, marketing magic for small biz owners. Publisher is a small biz consultant, radio show host, author and owner of the Biz Resource Site.
Type of Publication: Email newsletter
Frequency of Publication: Every 3-5 weeks
URL: http://www.bizresource.com
Advertising Format: classifieds, sponsorship
Subscribe Instructions: Email bizinfo@bizresource.com with FREE TIPS in the subject line.

The BizWeb E-Gazette

Okay, I know what you're thinking: "Sure, of course he's going to list his own publication near the top of the list!" Ah ha! Gotcha. This is an alphabetical listing. So there. I won't deny the fact that the alphabet *did* have something to do with selecting the name of my publication though. You see, I enjoy this preferential placement in many other listings as well. Just the type of savvy thinking you would come to expect from someone making a living marketing on the internet, right?

Anyway, here's the scoop on the gazette...

Editor/Publisher Name: JDD Publishing
Editor/Publisher Email Address: Mail@JDD-Publishing.com
Cost of Publication: FREE
Description: Since its birth in August of 1996, the gazette has quickly become a leading source of business information for netrepreneurs in now more than 45 countries. Weekly highlights include helpful internet marketing tips, feature articles and internet business classifieds. With 15,000 subscribers as of May 1997 it's no wonder that advertisers are flocking to this electronic publication. The gazette's circulation is composed primarily of home-based and small business owners.
Type of Publication: Email newsletter
Frequency of Publication: Weekly
URL: http://www.bizweb2000.com/sample.htm
Advertising Format: Classified advertising available in each issue and in our high profile sample issue at http://www.bizweb2000.com/sample.htm
Subscribe Instructions: To subscribe, send any email

message to Subscribe@JDD-Publishing.com

The Bulletin!
Editor/Publisher Name: Larry Rockwell, Rational Business Systems
Email Address: rbs@one-rbs-plaza.com
Cost of Publication: Free to individual subscribers; licensable to sysops, and other groups or organizations
Description: Simply the best mix of interesting and informative information! Web marketing, Sci-Fi/Fact, World Music, Cyber Businesses, humor, trivia, products/ services, and occasional guest articles.
Type of Publication: Email newsletter
Frequency of Publication: Bi-weekly (10th & 20th each month)
URL: http://One-RBS-Plaza.com/suite120.phtml
Advertising Format: Classified
Subscribe Instructions: mailto:subscribe@one-rbs-plaza.com

Business To Business Magazine
Editor/Publisher Name: Editor: Josephine Ducharme Publisher: A. MeKrae
Email Address: editor@business2business.on.ca
Cost of Publication: FREE
Description: Business To Business Magazine stresses today's business concerns, presenting strategies for marketing, money matters, computer and internet technology, the environment and other relevant business issues.
Type of Publication: Web zine
Frequency of Publication: 10 times per year

URL: http://www.business2business.on.ca/welcome.html
Advertising Format: Sponsorship
Subscribe Instructions: Free access to the web zine address with no registration required.

Business Opportunity Marketletter and General Business MarketLetter (2 separate newsletters)
Editor/Publisher Name: BusinessLink
Email Address: businesslink@businesslink.net
Cost of Publication: FREE
Description: Two very good electronic newsletters that offer paid advertising in the form of web site announcements and classified ads.
Type of Publication: Email newsletters
Frequency of Publication: Weekly
URL: http://www.businesslink.net
Advertising Format: Classifieds
Subscribe Instructions: To be added to the General Business MarketLetter list send an Email to BusinessLink@rome.servint.com and type ADD in the SUBJECT Heading. To be added to the Business Opportunity MarketLetter list send an Email message to "Subscribe@infofree.com"

BYB Tips
Editor/Publisher Name: Hal Croasmun
Email Address: ywf@eden.com
Cost of Publication: FREE
Description: BYB Tips is a daily email list that provides ideas on how to build and improve your business on the internet.

Type of Publication: Email newsletter
Frequency of Publication: Daily
URL: http://www.yourwebfuture.com/archiveindex.htm
Advertising Format: None
Subscribe Instructions: Email majordomo@eden.com and in the body include: subscribe byb

Computer Profits Electronic Newsletter
Editor/Publisher Name: Pearson Publishing
Email Address: jdpearson@wr.net
Cost of Publication: FREE
Description: Learn how to turn your personal computer into cash! An excellent resource for the home-based entrepreneur.
Type of Publication: Email newsletter
Frequency of Publication: Bi-weekly
URL: http://www.uran.net/pearson/whichnws.html
Advertising Format: None
Subscribe Instructions: send email to: jdpearson@wr.net. with SUBJECT: "subscribe"

CyberMessenger E'Zine
Editor/Publisher Name: Eric Snyder
Email Address: natinfo@epix.net
Cost of Publication: FREE
Description: What's cool and new on the net. Also, lots of net business info and free reports.
Type of Publication: Email newsletter
Frequency of Publication: Every Tuesday, Thursday, Friday
URL: http://www.geocities.com/wallstreet/9611
Advertising Format: classified advertising and press

releases
Subscribe Instructions: e-mail with "subscribe" in Subject field: natinfo@epix.net

Cyberphoenix Weekly
Editor/Publisher Name: Alfred Michael Arzt, CyberPhoenix
Email Address: success@freedom-mall.com
Cost of Publication: FREE
Description: Business newsletter focusing on marketing and advertising.
Type of Publication: Email newsletter
Frequency of Publication: Weekly
URL: N/A
Advertising Format: Classifieds
Subscribe Instructions: Send any email message to subscribe@freedom-mall.com - you'll receive the latest issue immediately and be added to the subscription list!

Daniel's InfoZene
Editor/Publisher Name: Editor: Daniel Deane
Editor/Publisher Email Address: ddeane@cdc.net
Cost of Publication: FREE
Description: General interest/public service ezine. internet tips, humor, recipes, disability advocacy, and more.
Type of Publication: Email newsletter
Frequency of Publication: Weekly
URL: http://ucando.com/n/asn4236224.html
Advertising Format: Classifieds
Subscribe Instructions: infozene-info@lofcom.com

DEMC's E-Magazine
Editor/Publisher Name: Direct Email Marketing Co.
Email Address: mail@demc.com
Cost of Publication: FREE
Description: This one is currently one of the biggest business related ezines on the net, with a very large subscriber base. A very professional ezine with excellent classified sections.
Type of Publication: Email Newsletter
Frequency of Publication: Twice weekly
URL: None
Advertising Format: Classifieds.
Subscribe Instructions: For information on subscribing, call 800-348-3454 or email mail@demc.com

The Downline Reporter On-Line
Editor/Publisher Name: Wayne Sutton
Email Address: wayne@interwealth.com
Cost of Publication: FREE
Description: MLM (multi-level marketing) and small business training newsletter
Type of Publication: Email newsletter
Frequency of Publication: Weekly
URL: www.interwealth.com/tdro.htm
Advertising Format: sponsorship
Subscribe Instructions: Email wayne@interwealth.com

Electronic Money Tree (Netrepreneur's Digest)
Editor/Publisher Name: Strong Opinions On Success
Email Address: soos@soos.com
Cost of Publication: Free on web - $3 on disk
Description: A monthly selection of articles written for

the home-based entrepreneur and the small business owner.
Type of Publication: Web Zine & Ebook
Frequency of Publication: Monthly
URL: http://www.soos.com/$tree
Advertising Format: Full web page, sponsorship, and classifieds.
Subscribe Instructions: Free on web- $36/year on disk.

Entrepreneur Weekly
Editor/Publisher Name: Cyber Media.
Email Address: sales@eweekly.com
Cost of Publication: FREE
Description: Devoted to internet marketing and business practices. Excellent articles every week.
Type of Publication: Email newsletter
Frequency of Publication: Weekly
URL: http://www.eweekly.com
Advertising Format: Classifieds
Subscribe Instructions: Send an email message directly to "eweekly-equest@cyberconinc.com" with the subject: subscribe.

Exposure!
Editor/Publisher Name: Adam J. Boettiger of Global Exposure™
Email Address: exposure@usa.net
Cost of Publication: FREE
Description: This Internet Marketing Newsletter is an excellent newsletter for online marketers. You're sure to learn many new online marketing tips and strategies!
Type of Publication: Email newsletter

Frequency of Publication: Weekly
URL: http://www.exposure-usa.com
Advertising Format: Sponsorship
Subscribe Instructions:
mailto:exposure@groupserver.revnet.com
In the BODY of your message, put: SUBSCRIBE

Frank Bauer's $1,000,000 Newsletter
Editor/Publisher Name: Frank Bauer
Email Address: FrankBaGer@aol.com
Cost of Publication: FREE
Description: The online resource for network marketers.
Type of Publication: Email newsletter
Frequency Of Publication: Bi-monthly
URL: N/A
Advertising Format: As of the writing of this publication, the newsletter was offering free classified ads.
Subscribe Instructions: Send email to FrankBaGer@aol.com (Subject: subscribe)

Fusion Marketing Express
Editor/Publisher: Paul Short
Email Address: pauls@octonline.com
Cost of Publication: FREE
Description: Fusion is dedicated to providing online marketers with useful, current information about how to market products and services on the internet and WWW.
Type of Publication: Email newsletter
Frequency of Publication: Weekly
URL: N/A
Advertising Format: classified ads
Subscribe Instructions: email pauls@octonline.com with

"SUBSCRIBE FUSION" in the subject line

G3 Gazette
Editor/Publisher Name: NetPower Publishing
Email Address: NPP@powerpub.com
Cost of Publication: FREE
Description: Featuring business success tips, multiple contests, various prizes, free offers, business building resources to help you profit - online and off - and resources for creating that professional web presence.
Type of Publication: Email newsletter
Frequency of Publication: Bi-monthly
URL: http://www.powerpub.com
Advertising Format: Free product/service showcasing.
Subscribe Instructions: Email NPP@powerpub.com and type SUBSCRIBE in the subject line.

Gator's Byte: Weekly Web Site Promotion & Internet Marketing Tips Column
Editor/Publisher Name: The Gator
Email Address: gator@sitepromoter.com
Cost of Publication: FREE
Description: Valuable web site promotion and internet marketing tips. Learn how to place your site high on search engines while doing searches to find what you want. Increase sales and hits to your site.
Type of Publication: Email newsletter
Frequency of Publication: Weekly
URL: http://www.gatorsbyte.com
Advertising Format: sponsorship coming eventually
Subscribe Instructions: To SUBSCRIBE: Send an email to gator@sitepromoter.com with the words "Subscribe

Gator" in the subject line.

Global-HomeBiz.com Update
Editor/Publisher Name: Lorrin L. Lee
Email Address: lorrin@global-homebiz.com
Cost of Publication: FREE
Description: A newsletter for homebiz entrepreneurs to start, succeed, profit and enjoy their global homebiz on the net.
Type of Publication: Email newsletter
Frequency of Publication: Bi-monthly.
URL: http://www.global-homebiz.com
Advertising Format: Free Ads
Subscribe Instructions: Go to http://www.global-homebiz.com/ghbu.html

HomeMoney Free Email Newsletter
Editor/Publisher Name: Gary Christensen
Email Address: GChrist95w@aol.com
Cost of Publication: FREE
Description: HomeMoney Newsletter desires to provide home-based business people with useful info, locations of unique web sites, helpful and inspirational articles, tips and business success secrets.
Type of Publication: Email newsletter
Frequency of Publication: Bi-monthly
URL: www.homeincome.com/homebiz/
Advertising Format: classified ads
Subscribe Instructions: Free to subscribe, cancel anytime. E-mail to Gapach97@aol.com with words "subscribe me" in subject or body.

The Home Office Commuter e-Newsletter
Editor/Publisher Name: O. R. Harder & Associates
Email Address: rick@homeofficecommuter.com
Cost of Publication: FREE
Description: A newsletter published for the home business owner.
Type of Publication: Email newsletter
Frequency of Publication: Monthly
URL: http://homeofficecommuter.com
Advertising Format: classified ads
Subscribe Instructions: Send an e-mail message to rick@homeofficecommuter.com and put the word SUBSCRIBE in the Subject field.

I-NET Biweekly
Editor/Publisher Name: Mr. L. Smith
Email Address: inet@mlweb.com
Cost of Publication: FREE
Description: An Entrepreneur's Newsletter to help you build a successful business on the net. It features articles by internet consultant and editor of I-NET, Mr. L. Smith.
Type of Publication: Email newsletter
Frequency of Publication: Bi-weekly
URL: http://www.mlweb.com/maec.htm
Advertising Format: Free classified ads, if qualified.
Subscribe Instructions: email mailing@mlweb.com

Internet Business Communications
Editor/Publisher Name: Steve Todd
Email Address: ibc@sar-net.com
Cost of Publication: FREE

Description: Small business, internet oriented newsletter. Articles, opinions, tips, quotes and a few ads. Giveaways, suggested surfing and contests.
Type of Publication: Email newsletter
Frequency of Publication: Weekly
URL: none
Advertising Format: Classified and larger Co-op ads
Subscribe Instructions: Send Email to ibc@sar-net.com with Subject: Subscribe

Internet Marketing Issues
Editor/Publisher Name: Terry Williams
Email Address: IMIPUB@intersuccess.com
Cost of Publication: FREE
Description: Covers marketing in the global environment, designed to promote marketing concepts and tips that are easily implemented, time tested and effective.
Type of Publication: Email newsletter and Web zine
Frequency of Publication: Bi-monthly
URL: http://www.intersuccess.com/imi/
Advertising Format: Sponsorship
Subscribe Instructions: Send an email to Subscribe-IMI@intersuccess.com

The Internet ONLINE Business Newsletter
Editor/Publisher Name: Clyde Reid
Email Address: Publisher@ReidNet.com
Cost of Publication: FREE
Description: Timely articles and tips directed at online business services, products and/or opportunities. It must be workable totally online to be in our ezine.

Type of Publication: Email newsletter
Frequency of Publication: Semi-monthly
URL: http://www.ReidNet.com
Advertising Format: Limited classified
Subscribe Instructions: Email your request to NewsList@ReidNet.com

NETrageouz! Marketing™
Editor/Publisher Name: Ana Hernandez - MTE Publishers
Email Address: mariani@icanect.net
Cost of Publication: FREE
Description: Insider Strategies for Killer Online and Offline Marketing. This one comes highly recommended by JDD Publishing. It's simply one of the best new marketing zines on the internet!
Type of Publication: Email newsletter
Frequency of Publication: Monthly
URL: N/A
Advertising Format: Classifieds
Subscribe Instructions: Subscribe by sending mailto:mariani@icanect.net Subject:NETrageouz!

The NETResults News Service
Editor/Publisher Name: Al Bredenberg Business Reports
Email Address: ab@copywriter.com
Cost of Publication: FREE
Description: NETResults is a free e-mail newsletter covering the world of Internet marketing and business. NETResults offers Internet business news, how-to reports, analysis and commentary.

Type of Publication: Email newsletter
Frequency of Publication: 2-3 times/month
URL: http://www.copywriter.com
Advertising Format: Sponsorship, classified
Subscribe Instructions: Email abnewsman@silverquick.com In the body of your message, type: join abnews <your e-mail address here> Type in your actual e-mail address.

Opportunity Digest
Editor/Publisher Name: Edward Walde
Email Address: SSee559@aol.com
Cost of Publication: FREE
Description: Focuses on the best Money Making Programs in the World. Includes on-line marketing tips and new opportunities added in each issue!
Type of Publication: Email newsletter
Frequency of Publication: Bi-weekly
URL: None
Advertising Format: Classified
Subscribe Instructions: email: SSee559@aol.com (subj. subscribe)

Opportunity Herald
Editor/Publisher Name: Randy DeMoville
Email Address: wasi2@ix.gen.com
Cost of Publication: FREE
Description: Business opportunity newsletter. It presents a forum for individuals to advertise or to subscribe for advertisements targeted to their interests.
Type of Publication: Email newsletter
Frequency of Publication: Weekly

URL: N/A
Advertising Format: Classifieds
Subscribe Instructions: Point your browser to http://www.wasi.com/herald/ or send an email requesting to be added to the list to... <wasi2@ix.gen.com>

Pizazz
Editor/Publisher Name: James R. Santa Maria
Email Address: pizazz@ultimate.org
Cost of Publication: FREE
Description: Moderated forum for the exchange of ideas regarding network marketing. Interesting articles are published weekly.
Type of Publication: Email newsletter
Frequency of Publication: Weekly
URL: http://www.bbac.com
Advertising Format: Classified
Subscribe Instructions: Mailto:majordomo@ultimate.org
In the body of your message put the following two words only: subscribe pizazz

Small Business Advisor Newsletter
Editor/Publisher Name: Dr R. Sullivan
Email Address: BOBS@ISQUARE.COM
Cost of Publication: FREE
Description: For the entrepreneur and small biz owner.
Type of Publication: Email newsletter
Frequency of Publication: Monthly
URL: http://www.isquare.com
Advertising Format: Classified and Sponsorship
Subscribe Instructions: Email bobs@isquare.com with subscribe in subject

SOHO BizAlert! (Formery IWatch NetBiz Alert!)
Editor/Publisher Name: Calvin Merrick
Editor/Publisher Email Address: tcgrp@ibm.net
Cost of Publication: FREE
Description: Information, resources, tips and techniques for small, home-based businesses and entrepreneurs.
Type of Publication: Email newsletter and Web zine
Frequency of Publication: Monthly
URL: http://www.iwatch.com/SOHO/sohoba.html
Advertising Format: Classified and Sponsorship
Subscribe Instructions: Send email to: bks@iwatch.com
In subject field, put: SOHO-SUB

Success Digest
Editor/Publisher Name: Michael E. Angier/Success Networks Int'l
Email Address: success@together.net
Cost of Publication: FREE
Description: Information, inspiration, and insight for fun-filled, successful living. Dedicated to helping people be more effective and fulfilled.
Type of Publication: Email newsletter
Frequency of Publication: Monthly
URL: http://www.together.net/~success
Advertising Format: Classified
Subscribe Instructions: send an email message to majordomo@webcoach.com with the words "subscribe sdigest-list" in the body (without quotes)

Successful Online Marketing
Editor/Publisher Name: Greg Landry, M.S.

Email Address: Greg@Landry.com
Cost of Publication: FREE
Description: Free, weekly, online newsletter with emphasis on marketing any type of business online.
Type of Publication: Email newsletter
Frequency of Publication: Weekly
URL: N/A
Advertising Format: classified
Subscribe Instructions: Email Greg@Landry.com with "subscribe marketing newsletter" in the message.

Tourbus
Editor/Publisher Name: Patrick Crispen and Bob Rankin
Email Address: BobRankin@MHV.net
Cost of Publication: FREE
Description: A free guided tour of the internet and World Wide Web. A virtual tour of cyberspace!
Type of Publication: Email newsletter
Frequency of Publication: Weekly
URL: http://ua1ix.ua.edu/~crispen/ and http://www.TOURBUS.com
Advertising Format: sponsorship
Subscribe Instructions: Send SUBSCRIBE TOURBUS Your Name to LISTSERV@LISTSERV.AOL.COM

VirtualBusiness.News
Editor/Publisher Name: Paul Myers
Email Address: arkham@buffnet.net
Cost of Publication: FREE
Description: Weekly small business newsletter. Covers topics across the range of small business concerns, with

regular exclusive columns, new business ideas and in-depth feature articles.
Type of Publication: Email newsletter
Frequency of Publication: Weekly
URL: http://www.virtualbusiness.net
Advertising Format: Classified; limited number per issue.
Subscribe Instructions: Send email to VBNews-request@MailList.net, with Subject: subscribe. To receive the latest issue *and* subscribe, send any email to arkham=vbn@buffnet.net

Web Marketing Today
Editor/Publisher Name: Wilson Internet Services, Dr. Ralph F. Wilson, Editor
Email Address: rfwilson@wilsonweb.com
Cost of Publication: FREE
Description: An excellent source for current web marketing trends and strategies.
Type of Publication: Email newsletter
Frequency of Publication: Tri-weekly
URL: http://www.wilsonweb.com
Advertising Format: Sponsorship
To subscribe send the message SUBSCRIBE WEB-MARKETING to majordomo@wilsonweb.com

Weekly Success Tip
Editor/Publisher Name: Jeffrey Spencer
Email Address: ssimail@ix.netcom.com
Cost of Publication: FREE
Description: Quick motivational business and personal success tips. Articles could cover internet marketing, self-improvement, business tips and more.

Type of Publication: Email newsletter
Frequency of Publication: Weekly
URL: http://www.choicemall.com/successstyles
Advertising Format: Classified
Subscribe Instructions: Send e-mail to ssimail@ix.netcom.com with "SUBSCRIBE" in subject heading.

Working Solo
Editor/Publisher Name: Terri Lonier
Email Address: solonews@workingsolo.com
Cost of Publication: FREE
Description: Tips, news, and insights about self-employment and small business issues.
Type of Publication: Email newsletter
Frequency of Publication: Monthly
URL: N/A
Subscribe Instructions: Simply send an email message directly to: solonews@workingsolo.com.

Worldprofit Worldgram Electronic Newsletter
Editor/Publisher Name: Dr. Jeffrey Lant
Email Address: webmaster@worldprofit.com
Cost of Publication: FREE
Description: Internet marketing tips and more.
Type of Publication: Email newsletter
Frequency of Publication: Monthly
URL: http://www.worldprofit.com
Advertising Format: classified
Subscribe Instructions: Visit http://www.worldprofit.com and follow the links.

Wireless Superhighway Newsletter
Editor/Publisher Name: Richard McCary, Wireless Superhighway
Email Address: Rich15@ix.netcom.com
Cost of Publication: FREE
Description: Free newsletter geared to marketing on the internet.
Type of Publication: Email newsletter
Frequency of Publication: Quarterly
URL: http://www.rexx.com/telcom/
Advertising Format: N/A
Subscribe Instructions: email wireless@rexx.com

Your-Biz Newsletter
Editor/Publisher Name: Bob Osgoodby
Email Address: yjrm21a@prodigy.com
Cost of Publication: FREE
Description: Geared toward the Small Business Community, the Newsletter presents timely articles, humor and technology trends. A must have for the Home Business entrepreneur.
Type of Publication: Email Newsletter
Frequency of Publication: Weekly
URL: http://pages.prodigy.com/business
Advertising Format: N/A
Subscribe Instructions: Go to the Web Page at http://pages.prodigy.com/business and click on subscribe - or send an E-mail requesting subscription to yjrm21a@prodigy.com

Your Business Newsletter
Editor/Publisher Name: Gabriel Nijmeh, GCN

Consultants
Email Address: gcn@interlog.com
Cost of Publication: FREE
Description: News, announcements, web site reviews and other helpful business related information is what you'll find in this great newsletter.
Type of Publication: Email newsletter
Frequency of Publication: Monthly
URL: http://www.interlog.com/~gcn
Subscribe Instructions: Email gcn@interlog.com with the word SUBSCRIBE YBN in the subject header.

I highly recommend you subscribe to most, if not all of these ezines. Not only will you gain some valuable knowledge on the subject of internet marketing, you'll discover some excellent new advertising venues.

If you're a writer, you now have an incredible resource of online publishers at your fingertips. Don't let it go to waste!

TIP: In addition to subscribing to the ezines listed in this publication, you should actively seek out other publications related to your area of expertise. Below are a few excellent sources on the web to find ezines. Remember, not only can you use these sites to ***find*** ezines, you can also use them to promote new mailing lists.

http://www.zinerack.com/
http://www.edoc.com/ejournal/
http://www.liszt.com/
http://www.meer.net/johnl/e-zine-list/

http://www.catalog.com/vivian/interest-group-search.html

In addition to checking these sources for ezines, it's a very good idea to subscribe to something called the "NEW-LIST announcement list." This list will keep you up to date on any changes to existing lists as well as announcing new lists as they become available.

To subscribe to the "NEW-LIST announcement list," send email to: LISTSERV@LISTSERV.NODAK.EDU with the words "Subscribe New-List" (no quotations) in the body of your message. (Be sure to disable your signature so you don't confuse the server.) You will then receive a confirmation message that you must reply to with the command "ok" (no quotations) in the body.

PHASE TWO:
WORKING THE WEB

Your marketing campaign is now well under way. You've set up your autoresponders with your sales messages and started e-marketing. By all means, don't stop there. So what's next? Get a web site!

Marketing on the World Wide Web is by far the most popular online marketing method. It can be very powerful, although the fact is, web marketing works better as your budget grows. Whether you're building your own site or putting one up in one of the popular web malls, web marketing requires heavy promotion.

This chapter is designed to teach you how to effectively build your World Wide Web presence from the ground up - without spending a fortune. If you're marketing in cyberspace you need to learn this stuff.

Although setting up shop on the web can seem like a daunting task, it really is no more difficult than getting your internet marketing campaign rolling. Take it a step at a time as it is presented. Here are the steps I will cover:

a. Finding someone to build your site or doing it yourself.
b. Designing a "marketing friendly" site.
c. Registering your domain.
d. Finding a host and setting up shop.
e. Promoting your site online.
f. Promoting your site offline.
g. Building traffic with our inside strategies.

FINDING A WEB SITE DESIGNER OR DOING IT YOURSELF

Naturally, the very first step in establishing your presence on the World Wide Web is building a web site. To achieve this task you must choose one of the following directions:

1. Hire someone outside of your company to construct your web site for you.

or...

2. Take on the task within your own company; which may ultimately mean constructing the web site yourself or with your co-workers.

I feel very strongly that choice number two is the way to go. This is a task that should be done in-house. As long as you or someone you work with has experience on a computer, web site construction and maintenance can be learned in a relatively short period of time.

I will admit that building my own web site seemed like quite a chore in the beginning. At times, I had serious doubts that I could learn this stuff at all. I was deathly afraid of hyper text markup language (html), which was necessary for me to learn before starting the task.

Then a great thing happened. Software companies started introducing web authoring software that worked like programs I already knew. I no longer needed to master html. Since I was familiar with Microsoft Word, I decided to purchase Microsoft FrontPage, which requires no html knowledge. For a little more than $100, I was exposed to my first experience with web site construction.

Within a month I had my site up and running on the web. Although it has gone through a constant state of evolution, the site that's on the web today is still very much like the site I uploaded that first day. Check it out when you get a chance: **http://www.bizweb2000.com**

If you're hedging on the issue of in-house webmastering versus contracting out, you must consider several factors. The following holds true if you hire another company to do your web site construction and maintenance:

- Web site construction can be **very expensive**. The bigger the site, the more it will cost.

- Designing site changes can be more time consuming and very costly.

- Making frequent changes to keep your web site fresh can be very costly.

- The knowledge you'll be passing up on can be more costly than the time and money lost.

If you take on the task yourself, you are free to make changes to your site anytime you wish. The changes will cost you nothing to implement, except time.

But beware, webmastering can be extremely time consuming, especially in the beginning. Expect to put in some long hours in front of the computer getting things just perfect.

But I believe that in the end, it is worth the time. Here are some helpful tips to get you started, so you too can conquer webmastering...

For starters, you would benefit from actually knowing a little html, since it is the source code behind all web authoring programs. Even when using one of the many web authoring programs, a basic knowledge in html will make small changes to your site easier.

To learn html, you can simply pick up one of the many books available on the subject. If you need some online assistance with your html, visit the Macmillan HTML Survival Guide on the Web at **http://www.mcp.com/general/workshop/survival/**.

There you'll find the answer to just about any html question you'll run into. They offer help for both beginners and advanced webmasters. They even have some templates available for you to download.

For those of you a little scared of html, fear not, there are plenty of easier roads to choose. Keep in mind, there are literally hundreds of different web authoring programs out there. This listing of excellent resources, contains some of the newer stuff available as of 1997:

PageMaker 6.5 by Adobe for Windows 95/NT and Mac. Professional publishing software for print and online pages. **http://www.adobe.com/prodindex/pagemaker/main.html**

HotDog Professional 3 by Sausage Software Designed specifically for Windows 95/NT. New 32-bit version of a very popular HTML Editor Shareware. **http://www.sausage.com.au/hotdog32.htm**

AOLpress by AOL for Windows 3.1, Windows 95/NT, Macintosh. Specifically designed for AOL users to make Web Site authoring easier on beginners. Freeware for AOL members. Go to their web site at **http://www.aolpress.com/press/index.html**

Microsoft FrontPage 97 Designed for Windows 95. For webmasters and novices alike. This version of Frontpage is available at **http://www.microsoft.com/frontpage/**

For the record, I decided to go with Microsoft Frontpage. This is by no means an endorsement for Mr. Gates. I simply decided that it would probably be easy to learn since I recently upgraded to Windows 95. Whatever your choice, remember, you've made a wise decision in becoming master of your own web.

Note: If you simply do not have the time to be a webmaster, yet want to save money on web site design, visit the following site: **http://www.bizweb2000.com/design.htm**

Although web site design is not a service I offer, I've posted this page to refer you to some low cost designers that I've used for spot work, such as logo and banner design.

HOW TO DESIGN A "MARKETING FRIENDLY" WEB SITE

Okay, you've made the decision to set up shop on the web. Whether you've heeded my advice and decided to build it yourself, or you've made the decision to hire someone else, you'll need to sit down and design your site. That's what this section will address.

You see, a marketing site - a site that's designed to sell something - needs some special consideration. Anyone can build a web site, but not everyone can build a site that makes money!

Rather than go into long discussions about the pro's and cons of each issue, I've decided to explain the most important components of a "marketing friendly" web site. If you follow at least 90 percent of them, your site will have an excellent chance at being profitable. Naturally, you'll need traffic too, but we'll give you the inside scoop on that later.

For now, let's concentrate on all the things you'll need to consider when designing your web site. Here are the top ten key components:

1. Offer valuable information.

Sounds like a no-brainer right? Well, it's not. Take a look on the World Wide Web. You'll find page after page of below par sales pitches disguised as web pages. They are not profitable. Your site must be built on the premise of content. This is the single most important thing to consider when designing your site. In order for people to visit and return to your site it must have value to them. You can provide value by offering free stuff. Offer free inside information about your area of expertise. Offer a free newsletter subscription. Hold contests. These are just a few ideas that create interest and keep it.

2. Keep your graphics to a bare minimum.

Graphics take time to load. People surfing the web are an impatient lot. They typically won't wait for images to load if it involves more than 15 seconds. Shrink the file size of all your graphics and they will load faster. This can be done by visiting the GIF Wizard from Raspberry Hill Publishing Inc. at **http://www.raspberryhill.com/gifwizard.html**

Use the ALT attribute in the image tags of all your graphics. Many people surf the web with images turned off. The ALT attribute will describe the content of your graphics and make site navigation easier and faster. It's as simple as adding into your image tags the following: alt="Your Description". For an example of what your code will look like, visit **http://www.bizweb2000.com/banners.htm** and check the tags that go with my banners.

3. If you're considering using frames when designing your site, don't - at least not until 1998 or later.

Frames divide web page content into sections, and look really cool. But the fact is, they load slowly and many older browsers simply cannot handle frames. As more people utilize current browsers, this won't be an issue. Remember, when you're designing a site with the intention of selling something, you need all the visitors you can get. Marketing will forever be a numbers game.

4. Make sure every page in your site has a quick hyperlink to your home page and every other area of interest.

Remember, many visitors will come in at a page other than your home page. You need to make navigation as simple as possible. A lost surfer is a lost customer.

5. At the top of any product/service page, give the option of retrieving the information via email from an autoresponder.

Not only does this show that you respect your visitors time restraints, it will allow you to email a follow-up message in a week or two.

6. Use simple fill-out forms to ease customer participation, such as surveys, questionnaires and other feedback forms.

A basic CGI "forms to email" application will do the trick. CGI stands for the "Common Gateway Interface," which is a standard for interfacing external applications with information servers, such as HTTP or Web servers. This allows visitors to fill out a form, click submit, and have the info delivered to you by email.

If you want to learn about CGI, or you're looking for a CGI program or script for your particular computer system or application, you should check out Yahoo's CGI directory at: **http://www.yahoo.com/Computers/world_wide_web/CGI_Common_Gateway_Interface/**

If you're looking to add a fill-out form to your site without going through the CGI learning curve, visit David Beroff's forms to email generator at **http://www.note.com/success/public/freeform/?BizWeb** and have one generated for you automatically. You just fill out the form at their site and their server creates the code for you to use on your web site. It also handles the submissions when someone fills out the form at your site and automatically sends it to the email address you specify in a neatly formatted message. This resource is simple to use and it's free.

7. Spice up your pages with a few animated GIFS.

These graphics keep your audience interested. When using animated GIFS, use no more than four on any single page if possible. Some older browsers have been known to crash when encountering five or more animated GIFS on a single web page.

8. Offer as many methods of ordering as possible.

Visitors to your pages should have the option of (a) printing an order form (preferably a separate web page that formats easily onto one printed page) (b) copy/pasting an order form into their email program and emailing their order, or (c) faxing the order form to your fax number. These options may sound obvious, but you'd be surprised how many limited order forms I've run across.

9. Offer the option of ordering from a secure server.

If you've been marketing online for any length of time, you realize the hottest topic involving internet commerce has been security, especially among the media. Although using credit cards to make purchases online is actually very safe, a common myth has been that it is not.

The fact is, secure transaction technology has been in place for a while now. All major Web browsers now support Secure Sockets Layer (SSL) technology and many web servers are also compatible. The lack of security comes into play when credit card details are emailed from the web server to the vendor. (An encryption standard for this should be in place sometime in 1997.)

Secure transactions *are* possible with today's technology. I use ShopCart™ to collect secure profits. ShopCart allows me to have secure ordering for as many products as I need, all at one low rate. Credit card details wait at their web server until I pick them up through my browser, insuring completely secure transactions for my customers. Check out a demo at: **http://www.shopcart.com**

10. Keep your site content fresh.

This gets overlooked far too often. If someone visits your web site and finds that nothing has changed since the last time they visited, chances are they will never return. Avoid this scenario by updating your content weekly or monthly at the bare minimum. (Hey, I told you webmastering can turn into some long hours!)

That about does it for "marketing friendly" site guidelines. If you follow these recommendations closely, you'll increase the likelihood of your web site making money.

MASTER OF YOUR OWN DOMAIN

Once you've built your web site, you'll need to make an important decision. You must decide whether or not to get your own domain name.

My best recommendation to you is DO IT.

Getting your own domain name is an excellent tool that immediately gives your business a professional and internet-established presence.

Many people consider this a necessity for only very large companies. Actually, when you look at the benefits you get by doing it, you'll see that it's well worth the $50 yearly cost.

The first benefit is an obvious one - identity. Instead of your email address being recognized as a user or subscriber (xxx@aol.com or yyyy@compuserve.com) to an internet access provider, you will have your own identity. When people email you at anything@yourcompany.com they will have the feeling they are contacting one of those large companies. *Sounding* like an established business certainly goes a long way in marketing.

In addition, your web site address (URL) will look like "http://www.YourCompany.com" instead of something like this, http://members.aol.com/joeblow. This also tells your prospects you mean business.

The other big benefit is that you can now have all of your email correspondence broken down to the specific departments of your business. Now your email address will be *anything*@yourcompany.com. You tell prospects they can email their orders to order@yourcompany.com or to send inquiries to staff@yourcompany.com. This not only helps organization on your end, it also again presents that large company image.

There are many companies on the net that offer a domain name registration service. Unfortunately, many businesses are being taken advantage of in this area. Too many companies are charging an exorbitant amount for this service. It should not be an expensive undertaking.

You can even take on the chore yourself, although I must warn you, it isn't a simple procedure for the inexperienced. You may be better off having a company with some experience in this area handle domain name registration for you. Anyway, here's the site for you do-it-yourselfers:

http://rs.internic.net/help/domain/

To see if the domain name you want is available, visit: **http://www.bizweb2000.com/freehelp.htm**

I've placed a banner at the top of that page which will do the search for you. From there you can also use our handy registration services and reserve the name of your choice.

When registering your domain name, you will be required to pay one hundred dollars to InterNIC. This is the organization that handles all domain name matters. This fee covers the first two years. After that you will be billed fifty dollars per year. Well worth the price! Remember though, the names are going fast! The sooner you get started, the more likely you are to get the name you request.

FIND A HOST AND SET UP SHOP

The next step in your web marketing campaign is to find a company to host your web site. If you decided against getting your own domain name, more than likely you will not need to worry about finding a host. Chances are you will simply host your web pages right on the server that provides internet access for you.

For instance, if you are diehard AOL user (there are millions out there) and you are starting to market your wares on the internet, you may simply decide that the extra expense of domain registration and web hosting is not for you just yet. In this case you can utilize AOL's "My Place" section to upload your web site. Even if you have created the site using an html editor other than AOL's you simply upload the html file to their server.

Like AOL, many major online access providers and ISP's now offer a decent amount of server space for hosting your web pages. Even if you do decide to host your pages elsewhere, I highly recommend using any "free" space your provider offers. (I'll explain why when I teach you a nice little trick in an upcoming section.)

Note: You can host your web site with most web hosting companies *without* getting your own domain name. This is usually referred to as a non-virtual account and your web address would look something like this: http://www.webhostcompany.com/yourname. Although this will save you the InterNic fees and a few dollars each month on hosting charges, you'll lose the valuable name recognition factor of having your own domain. (Am I starting to get across the importance of owning your own domain?)

If you are going the wise route of getting your own domain name, you'll need a host for your web site. Although many ISP's offer domain registration and web hosting, it's a good idea to shop around before assuming your ISP is the way to go.

The hardest thing about finding a host for your site is getting started. That's where the following information comes in, which will prove invaluable when you decide to start shopping for a web site host. This site, new as of 1997, will save you hours and hours of searching and frustration. Visit "The Ultimate Web Host List" at: **http://www.webhostlist.com**.

Thanks to this site, shopping for a web site host has never been easier. With literally thousands of companies now offering web hosting services, it had become a major chore sorting through them all to find the best deal. Their monthly "Top 25" makes finding a web host simple, even for the inexperienced. It lists the best hosts on the internet by different criteria including price, access, space and speed.

Remember to be careful when considering price. Many hosting companies charge a small monthly fee ranging from $14.95 to $24.95 and then charge more based on bandwidth. What this means is that when your web site traffic increases, you will pay more money for hosting.

Also make sure your server has high-speed access. When it comes to speed, you should settle for no less than a T3 connection. Sacrificing quality for lower cost web hosing, can prove fatal to any online business.

Before you decide on a host for your site, read my report at **http://www.bizweb2000.com/virtual.htm**. It will save you lots of time, money and aggravation.

Once you've decided on a host you'll need to get your web site up on their server. This is usually accomplished by means of File Transfer Protocol (FTP). In my case it's even simpler since I use Microsoft Frontpage and the "publish web" command is right on my file menu. Whatever means you're using, the web hosting company you go with should be more than happy to walk you through the process the first few times. There's really not much to it once you've done it a few times.

If you need some assistance with FTP, here's a helpful site to visit: **http://www.ipswitch.com/Support/FAQ/ws_ftp.html**

Test All The Angles

Once your site is up, be sure to test all the angles. By all the angles I'm referring to how your site looks when viewed through different browsers.

For the most part, the internet population is currently using three browsers. I realize there are more than three browsers in the world, however, the lion's share involves the big three - Netscape Navigator, Microsoft Internet Explorer and AOL's browser.

When your site is nearing its final stages of completion, *before* you start telling people about it, test the site from each of these three major browsers. It may look great when viewed from one or two of them, but horrible in the other. These problems usually come into play when using multiple tables at your site. (Tables are commonly used to divide content into sections, or cells, for the purpose of rearranging text and pictures on your page.)

If you do not have access to all three of these different browsers, contact a friend or associate who does. Have them visit your site and check each and every page for layout problems. After all, when someone visits your web site and sees that you have some major flaws, they are not likely to stick around, much less buy something from you.

I even went as far as checking my site using different versions of the browsers I mentioned. Remember, many people do not upgrade their software as often as you might. If you have access to some older versions, check your site with them. You may be surprised at what you find.

If your friends can't help, try Bobby. Bobby is a simple to use program that serves two purposes. It will help you make your web pages accessible to those with disabilities, and it will also find these html compatibility issues that prevent pages from displaying correctly on different web browsers. Visit **http://www.cast.org/**

bobby/ and see what your site will look like from all the major browsers and different versions of each.

You simply fill in a form with the URL of a web page that you want Bobby to examine. Select a browser that you want the web page to be compatible with, and press the Submit button. Bobby does the rest.

Remember, although it is virtually impossible to make your site look great from every version of every browser, it is certainly worth making an effort. If your site is easily viewed and navigated from all three of the major browsers, you will have a higher number of happy visitors, which will result in more purchasing customers!

WEB SITE PROMOTION

AN ONGOING TASK

So you've got your web site up and running. What's next? How about drumming up a little business?

What good is a web site if you don't get any visitors? I would like to share with you how to avoid the single biggest mistake made by "almost made it" netrepreneurs. It happens all the time...

Too many people spend more energy designing and building their web sites thinking that this is the most important part of putting their business on the web. It is not!

The most important part of your online marketing campaign is the actual marketing!

This means that you MUST spend the bulk of your efforts promoting your new web site. Once you accept this fact, you will be started on your road to online success.

In the next few sections I will describe the best ways to attract visitors to your site, including my powerful nine-step plan to bring traffic to your site and keep customers coming back.

First you will learn the five things you should be doing *online*. Then you'll learn the four steps to promoting your site in the "real world" or *offline*.

Finally, I will teach you some of the tricks of the trade. These are the most closely guarded secrets on web site promotion.

After you read this information do yourself a favor and read it again. The information you'll learn will be invaluable to your web marketing campaign.

ONLINE WEB SITE PROMOTION

Naturally, the best place to start promoting your web site is where it exists, on the internet. Below you'll find some of the "musts" when promoting your web site online. If you're not doing *all* of this stuff, you'd better be doing *most* of it. Here's what you'll learn:

1. Search Engine And Directory Submissions
2. Banner Advertising Techniques and Strategies
3. Free Publicity through Ezines & Discussion Lists
4. Publishing An Email Newsletter
5. Online Press Releases

1. Search Engine and Directory Submissions

Submit your new web address to the hundreds of search engines and directories on the web. This will allow people searching on a specific subject to find your site.

You can use a submission service or do it yourself. A few of the more popular URL submission services are SubmitIt (**http://www.submit-it.com**) and Exploit (**http://www.exploit.com**). Before deciding to use these services, make sure your site is ready to go. This includes reviewing and implementing all of the tips included in the rest of this section.

Whether you're doing it yourself or hiring someone else, make sure your URL gets listed with all of these major players:

Alta Vista: **http://www.altavista.digital.com/**
Excite: **http://www.excite.com**

Hotbot: **http://www.hotbot.com**
Infoseek: **http://www.infoseek.com**
Lycos: **http://www.lycos.com**
Starting Point: **http://www.stpt.com/**
Webcrawler: **http://www.webcrawler.com**
Yahoo: **http://www.yahoo.com**

2. Banner Advertising Techniques and Strategies

Get some banners made and posted at similar web sites. Although banner advertising on sites like Yahoo or other popular search engines can be very expensive, it is not necessary to spend a fortune when advertising with banner ads on the web. Anyone can take advantage of banner advertising and when done properly, it can be a cost effective way to bring traffic to your site.

Designing your own banners has recently gotten much easier. Many retail software stores now offer inexpensive software packages dedicated solely to banner creation. If you prefer to get fancy on your own, check out this hot new tool, "Banner Show" by Web Genie. This program allows you to create your own rotating banner show quickly and easily: **http://www.webgenie.com/Software/Banner/**

If you'd like to design a few banners *without* purchasing software, you can visit The Banner Generator by Coder.com. This excellent web resource is simple and fun to use: **http://www.coder.com/creations/banner/**

Here are a few things to consider when designing your banners:

a. Try to keep them between 5K to 10K in size. The faster your banner loads, the more likely it is to be seen.

b. Use short action phrases on your banners. Although more than a few net vets have been hammering banners that say "Click Here" or "Click on Over," the fact remains that banners with these phrases are more effective.

c. Use animated banners when you can. They are more effective than non-animated, or static banners.

d. Remember to use the ALT attribute (described in detail on page 64).

If you have neither the time nor inclination to design your own banners, here are three places to get FREE Banners for your business-related web site:

AAAA Banner Creation Service
http://jeffrey.simplenet.com/banner/index.html
Free for commercial and non-commercial sites, only requirement is a link to their site using the code they provide.

NIS Designs
http://www.10mb.com/nis/features.html
Offers free banners for businesses. Visit them and check out some samples. Nearly 100 various demonstrations.

Spacebar Solutions
http://members.tripod.com/~spacebar/

Offers free banners for businesses-related web sites. All they require is a link to their site.

As far as getting your banners into the action, there are many ways to get them up onto other pages. You should consider joining The Internet Link Exchange and BannerSwap:

http://www.linkexchange.com
http://www.bannerswap.com

These two sites give you the opportunity to swap links with other web marketers based on a credit system. You earn credits each time you show a banner at your site. As credits add up, you receive exposures at other sites.

Another great way to get your banners up at other sites is by doing a little swapping with some other web marketers.

Here's a method I've used to get links to high-traffic sites related to mine. Go to your favorite search engine, I like to use multi-search engines like DogPile (see **http://www.bizweb2000.com/engines.htm**), and search on the keywords related to your site. Visit the first 25 to 30 sites that come up. These sites should all have a good amount of traffic since they've managed to get listed high up in the search engines. (Something you'll learn in the next chapter.) Next, send an email message to the webmaster at each of the sites that look decent, similar to the following message I've used with great success:

Hello There! (Personalize whenever possible)

Just visited your site for the first time today. Fantastic.

I've been "working the web" for almost a year now and I can't imagine a better way to make a living. Perhaps you'd like to swap banner ads with us?

Your visitors may be very interested in our free "BizWeb Gazette".

We'd be more than happy to place a reciprocal link to your site. Have a look-see when you get a chance.

http://www.bizweb2000.com/sample.htm

Regards, Jim Daniels

JDD Publishing - Home of "The BizWeb E-Gazette!"

Another method that works well is to hold monthly contests at your site and offer some free stuff. Hold "Link To Us" contests with valuable giveaways. Whatever it is you are marketing, many of your web site patrons would almost certainly like a chance at getting it for free. Tell them all they have to do is put one of your banners on their page and they'll be entered into your monthly contest.

I even post a variety of banners at my site so they can choose the one they like. Visit **http://www.bizweb2000.com/banners.htm** and take a look. Notice that I've made it as simple as possible for people to link to my site by giving explicit details on how to do it.

Every month when you draw your winner, be sure to post the information at your site. Let others see what a great prize the person has won. Even more people will want in and your links will add up fast!

3. Free Publicity through Ezines and Discussion Lists

In addition to actually paying for advertising in online newsletters or ezines, there is a very simple way to receive *free* publicity.

Whatever you are selling, you hopefully know plenty about it. You can establish yourself as an authority on the subject by offering free advice on the topic. Once you put together some valuable information, simply email it to the publishers of your favorite ezines in the form of short articles and tip submissions.

I've been using this method for quite awhile now with excellent results. Every month (scheduled like clockwork, so it gets done) I submit a new article to the publishers of all my favorite ezines. I simply include a short four- or five-line *footer* or *resource box* at the end of each article. This footer resembles my signature file and includes my autoresponder addresses and URL. If you're not already doing this, I highly recommend it.

In addition to ezines, there are a growing number of discussion lists on the internet. A discussion list is usually delivered via email like an ezine, but differs from an ezine in one major way - discussion lists allow you to voice your opinion, usually through a moderator. There are discussion lists on many subjects and they're a great way to get answers to specific questions about your particular area of interest.

These discussion lists hold a marketing value similar to that of newsgroups. You help others while your sig file does your marketing. Discussion groups are much more powerful though, since they are delivered to a targeted audience, rather than having to find them. Many discussion groups offer advertising as well, usually in the form of sponsorships.

One of my personal favorites is Adam J. Boettiger's I-Advertising Digest: **http://www.exposure-usa.com/i-advertising/**

This is a moderated, global discussion on internet advertising, marketing and online commerce. Issues are also posted to the Web at: **http://www.exposure-usa.com/i-advertising/archives.html**

You can subscribe to this discussion group by sending a message with the word "subscribe" in the body of the message to mailto:I-advertising@groupserver.revnet.com

If you're interested in online advertising, I highly recommend you subscribe to this list.

Here are a few great sites to locate discussion lists on any topic imaginable:

http://www.neosoft.com/internet/paml/bysubj.html An excellent list indexed by subject.

http://www.lsoft.com/lists/listref.html
A list of 12,000+ lists which also contains the number of subscribers to each list.

http://www.liszt.com/
A list of over 71,000+ lists that is very easy to use.

http://www.webcom.com/impulse/list.html

A list of lists courtesy of Impulse Research.

4. Publishing An Email Newsletter

I started my email newsletter, The BizWeb E-Gazette in August of 1996. Originally, I started it because I figured I could sell a few classified ads each week. Little did I know, my ezine would become my number one tool in promoting my web site and my own products and services. If you are not already publishing your own email newsletter, I highly recommend you do so.

Publishing an email newsletter is not difficult. Aside from the reason I just mentioned, there are plenty more reasons why you should consider starting your own "zine." Here are just a few:

- Your customers/prospects won't have to find you. They'll constantly be "in touch" and in tune with your business.
- You can keep your own customers/prospects abreast of new products and services as they become available.
- You can make money offering classified or sponsorship advertising if you wish.
- It is the cheapest form of promotion you'll ever find! Unlike traditional newsletters, there are no printing or postage costs.
- Since your own cost is zero, you can offer free subscriptions thus insuring a steady flow of new prospects.

Should you decide you want to give it a shot, here's how to get started...

Select a good email program. I prefer Eudora Pro by Qualcomm. Qualcomm is a steady company currently trading on NASDAQ. Although there are close to a hundred different choices in email programs, (I've tried a handful), Eudora seems to be the easiest to configure and use. It also has a built-in feature that lets you mail to a large number of email addresses at once.

If you don't want to buy the Pro version which is available in software stores, you can download a free version called Eudora Light at their web site: **http://www.eudora.com**

Once you have your email program set up and configured, practice mailing to a few people at once by pasting a few addresses into the "nickname" field. (Eudora calls it this, other programs like Pegasus call it a "distribution list".) Next, send a message to yourself and put your list in the BCC (blind carbon copy) field. It's important to use the BCC field when mailing to a list. This insures that everyone on the list does not see all the other email addresses on the list. No one wants their email address publicized all over the net.

If you need more detailed instruction on this procedure, visit my home page at **http://www.bizweb2000.com**. There you'll find a low cost manual that goes into far more detail for someone who is just learning these skills.

After you've perfected your skills all you need is some email addresses to send your newsletter to. I can even set you up with this too!

Here's what you do: Compose an email message that tells people about your newsletter and email it to the NewList Announcement List. If you want you can use the template below. This is the actual announcement I sent to promote my newsletter. Just replace the name, details and contact information with your own.

From: "BizWeb E-Gazette" <Mail@JDD-Publishing.com>

Subject: NEW: The BizWeb E-Gazette!

To: NEW-LIST@LISTSERV.NODAK.EDU

"The BizWeb E-Gazette!" via FreeNewsletter@JDD-Publishing.com

"The BizWeb E-Gazette!" is a free email newsletter delivered every Friday.

Here you'll discover revealing online marketing tips, feature articles from entrepreneurs making their living online, news, and business related classifieds.

This newsletter is specifically designed for netrepreneurs. If you're interested in staying informed on low cost effective internet marketing strategies, this newsletter is for you!

A few previous articles include:

"Can You Really Make A Living On The Internet?"

"The Power of Email Marketing!

"The Ezine Explosion!"

"Effective Internet Advertising Techniques"

To start your FREE E-Mail Subscription to JDD Publishing's "BizWeb E-Gazette", send mailto:FreeNewsletter@JDD-Publishing.com and type: SUBSCRIBE in the subject line.

Owner: Jim Daniels <Mail@JDD-Publishing.com> <http://www.bizweb2000.com>

That's it. But make sure you're ready to handle a boatload of email messages before you post your announcement. Within a few days of posting my announcement, I received about 400 new subscribers, and you should too. More requests continued to trickle in for weeks, bringing the total to more than 500 new subscribers from a single email message!

5. Online Press Releases

Yet one more way to promote your business online is by sending a press release. Below is an excellent source to accomplish this sometimes daunting feat.

Multimedia Marketing Group's Internet News Bureau: http://www.newsbureau.com/

Multimedia Marketing Group
Tel: (888) 699-6939 or (503) 699-6939
Email: mailto:info@newsbureau.com

For a reasonable fee they'll email 1,200+ online media outlets that have asked for such releases. This is an excellent way to notify the media of new products and services.

Well, that sums up the online marketing section. Just remember, like traditional marketing, online marketing involves many aspects. Sample the many different methods available and stick with what works best for you. Now we'll move into some effective ways to market your web site offline, or in the real world.

OFFLINE WEB SITE PROMOTION

Since this book is about online marketing, I won't go wild explaining how to promote your business offline. However, since it *is* important to promote your site in the real world, I will cover the basics. I'll also point out some great online resources for offline promotion. Be sure your business is actively marketing offline by doing most, if not all of the following:

1. List Cyber-info on everything that leaves your office
2. Articles and press releases
3. Traditional advertising
4. Direct Mail

1. Promote on business cards and everything else that leaves your office

This is a must. You absolutely must put your email address and your URL on every piece of literature that leaves your office. This includes business stationery, envelopes, invoices, sales literature and especially your own and your employees' business cards. Below is a good example:

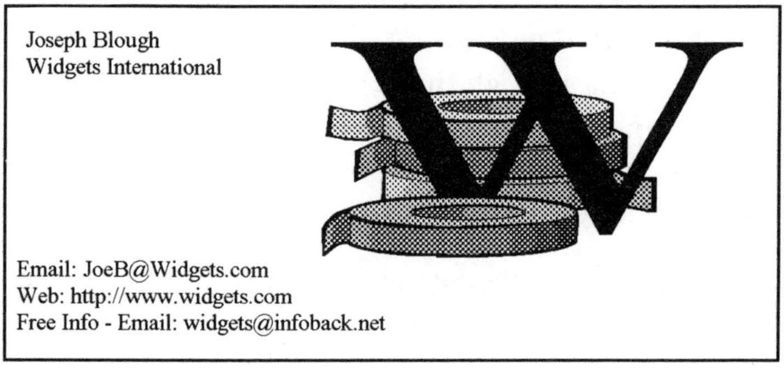

Note that this business card also contains an autoresponder address. This is an excellent way to promote your business. Anyone holding your business card can instantly receive information about your products and services via email, any time of the day, any day of the year. What a tool!

Remember, anything that goes out of your office should have your important cyberspace contact information. Start this little project today.

2. Articles and press releases

Just like online, writing and submitting articles and press releases is an excellent way to get free publicity. Tell the world about your new stuff as it is introduced. Familiarize people with your type of product or service by writing short articles about the basics of your area of expertise. Once you have something professional together, visit this site: **http://www.gebbieinc.com/presto.htm**

Here you'll find America's weekly newspapers and television stations broken down by state. They're even formatted for instant labels! Gebbie Press also offers a complete television database as well as more than 1,000 emails for radio and about 400 emails for television stations, all for free at their site. They also have email addresses and toll-free phone numbers for about 575 daily newspapers. In short, some terrific resources for publicity, at no cost.

Here are a few other great "real world" press release

resources on the web:

Automated Press Releases - http://www.gapent.com/pr/
Send press releases to more than 6,500 personalized publication contacts (not merely "editor"). You identify the industry; they write the press release.

BullsEye Internet News Service - http://www.bullseyeinc.com/docs/pricing.html
Corporate release posting package for public relations professionals.

PR NewsTarget - http://www.newstarget.com/blastnow.htm

3. Traditional advertising

In addition to getting the word out in the form of articles and press releases, you should seriously consider paying for some advertising.

When advertising in traditional publications it is very important to remember the basics. Since this book is *not* intended to teach traditional marketing strategies, I will only touch briefly on this subject and offer a few online resources.

The most important thing to consider in every form of advertising is selecting the proper location for your ads. You must concentrate your efforts on your target audience. Once you have decided who you are trying to reach, find out what types of publications your audience is most likely to read.

Instead of focusing solely on major magazines with their very high advertising rates, look into smaller publications like specialized newsletters, magazines, and trade publications. There are many specialized publications available that pertain to just about every business, occupation, sport and hobby. The advertising rates are substantially lower in these specialty publications even though the circulation is not as large as the major magazines and newspapers. The readers of the smaller publications consist almost exclusively of your target audience.

If you do plan to utilize traditional advertising, you can get a handle on the media resources by checking out Standard Rate and Data Services (SRDS) on the web: **http://www.srds.com/index.html**

SRDS publications and directories have been the foundation of every solid media buy for more than 78 years - they are the "meeting place" where the nation's buyers and sellers of media converge and millions of dollars are exchanged daily.

Their innovative e-kit provides electronic access to media kit information for the leading publishers of business publications, consumer magazines and newspapers. These directories list business, technical, and trade publications categorized by markets served. You will find it very helpful when you are trying to decide where to advertise.

A few more resources for traditional advertising include:

http://www.tradepub.com/
The premier internet service for professional trade publications. Great for finding and subscribing to quality professional magazines.

http://www.magamall.com/
Magazine Newsstand displaying hundreds of Newsstand magazines and features more than 1,000 magazine publications available to consumers today. You can search for a magazine publication by title or by category.

4. Direct Mail

Many small businesses rely heavily on direct mail. Although it's not as cheap as direct *email*, you can reach a very targeted audience with a good list. Below are a few of the best direct mail resource sites on the web:

The National Mail Order Association:
http://www.nmoa.org/
Billed as the "HUB" of Direct Response Marketing for small and midsize firms. A great place for business information and contacts concerning mail order marketing, catalog marketing, database marketing, direct mail marketing or lead generation.

CyberDirect:
http://www.CyberDirect.com
Exclusively for direct marketers looking for mail services, mailing lists, fulfillment, computer services, printers, lettershops or anything relating to direct mail. CyberDirect bills itself as the direct marketing community's first stop on the internet.

CREATING A TRAFFIC JAM - INSIDER TRAFFIC BUILDING TIPS

Okay, time to get into some of the fun stuff. During the last year or so I've managed to scrounge quite a few traffic building tips from a number of credible sources. Most of the tips have to do with search engine placement. I'd like to share these tips with you and answer the most commonly asked question by web marketers: "How can I get my web pages to appear at the top of the search engines?"

It would be great if I could give you a one-word, or one-sentence answer. It's not that simple, but as you'll learn in the next 20 or so pages, it CAN be done.

If you've been on the net for any length of time, I'm sure you've seen plenty of sources selling "search engine secrets" for $20 to $50 or more. Usually delivered in an email message, these inside secrets really don't tell you all that much. How do I know? Well, let's just say I had to purchase a few of these reports for "research" purposes.

The fact is, most of these secrets weren't secrets to me at all. The reports I saw teach you how to "trick" the search engines by repeating your "keywords" - words relevant to your site - over and over on your pages. Then you match the color of this text to your background. So I tried it. Did it work? Well, it did for a short time until everyone started doing it. Then the major search engines starting penalizing for it and even pulling the pages that employed this tact. Beyond that, most of the stuff I saw in these "secret reports" consisted of nothing more than what I already learned from viewing the html source of pages with high placement. (This is easy. If you don't know how, you'll learn later on.)

An intelligent internet marketer knows that there is really no ONE way to beat these search engines at their own game. You can try new tricks as they come along, and perhaps win brief high placement once in a while, or you can rely on the proven strategies, which I am about to discuss. These strategies are guaranteed to improve your search engine positioning.

Once you get through the basic things you need to know, I'll provide you with some additional tactics. Many of the tactics you'll learn have allowed me to enjoy a long run at the top of some of the best search engines on the web.

1. Select a beneficial site title

What's in a name? Everything when it comes to online marketing!

Your site title is usually the first thing people see. If you choose a title that piques the curiosity of web surfers, you'll receive many more page hits.

Example: Which site of these two would you go to first?

a. Internet Marketing: Product sales and advertising studies.

b. All New: Revealing Internet Marketing Strategies and Tips!

More than likely, you would chose the second site. The

content may be the same at each site, however, the title lures more people to the second site. Why? People instinctively have a curious and emotional nature. They want to learn something new every day. They get excited when they see a chance to get their hands on some fresh information.

Also, you'll notice that the second title has something else going for it. Want to take a guess what that certain something might be?

It's the first word of the title. Many search engines and directories still rely on alphabet listing to decide which pages in a particular subject are listed first. Although this is not as big a factor as it was, say a year ago, it still comes into play. Just visit Yahoo.com and do a little poking around. You'll see exactly what I mean.

Remember this: In addition to containing some of the key elements I am about to explain, the name you choose for every one of your web pages should be original and intriguing.

Technical note: The title tag in your html code looks like this: <title> your dynamic name </title>

2. Keywords

Keywords are words that describe the content of your web page or site. There are a few different ways that keywords can bring traffic to your site.

As you are probably aware, when someone is surfing the web and decides to search on a certain topic, such as "ezine advertising," keywords play a major role in deciding which pages pop up first. Although there are other criteria that play an important role in the search engines' feedback, keywords are very important.

So how do you get the most out of keywords?

The first way is when you register your site with the various search engines and directories on the internet. Many of these sites will ask you to provide some keywords that describe your site.

It is important for you to take a few hours and think up some keywords that are relevant to your site. Try to come up with about 40 or so. Although you won't be able to use all 40 at each place you register, you should have that many on hand. Once you have a list compiled, start breaking it down into the best 30, the best 25, the best 10 and the best five words. Among your best keywords, be sure to mix in the plural version of each, as well as the capitalized words.

For example: Ezine,ezine,Ezines,ezines

Once you've compiled these lists, save them as a text or ASCII file that you can easily retrieve. As you submit your site to each of the search engines and directories, you'll be ready with a list of relevant keywords to paste into their forms.

If you're wondering what the most commonly searched words or phrases on the web are, here's a nice site to visit:

http://www.eyescream.com/dogpiletop200.htm

There you'll see a side-by-side comparison of the top 200 search words in a new search engine that has been doubling in size during early 1997. Beware, there's some pretty racy stuff there, as you might imagine.

The second way to utilize keywords is not quite as direct although just as important. The way many of the popular search engines and directories index pages is by checking for instances of relevant keywords *in the pages themselves.*

For example, if the words "ezine advertising" appear together throughout your web page many times, you stand an excellent chance of having your page pop up near the top of the list when someone searches on these two words. For this reason it is important to repeat your keywords as often as "naturally" possible throughout your web pages.

Remember though, the practice of repeating your keywords over and over, hundreds of times on a page, in order to force a positive placement no longer works. Nearly all search engines and directories have now installed countermeasures against this practice. They simply deny listing or penalize when a page with these qualities is submitted. (There are a few ways to be creative, as I'll get to in a moment.)

The third location your keywords come into play are in your META tags, which are described in detail next.

3. META Tags

META tags are not any big secret, but you need be

aware of them and understand how they work.

It is very important to insert META tags into all of your web pages since some of the more popular search engines rely on these tags. (AltaVista and Infoseek to name a couple.)

The META tags you use tell the search engines two things:

a) The description of your web page(s).

b) The keywords relevant to your page(s).

If you know html, you probably know how to use meta tags. However if you're using one of the many web authoring software programs now on the market, inserting META tags can be tricky.

As a Microsoft Frontpage user, I fall into that category. Therefore, I'll use my own experience as an example.

The newest version of FrontPage lets me edit html code from inside the program. No problem. However, the previous version (like many other web authoring programs) did not offer this option. Here's how I overcame this hurdle.

Using Windows Notepad, I opened up each .htm file in my Web and inserted the following lines of text between "<head>" and "</head>"

<meta name= "description" content= "My Page Description">

<meta name= "keywords" content= "my keywords">

Naturally, you'll be replacing "My Page Description"

with "your page description" and "my keywords" with "your keywords" relevant to your pages. Leave the rest of the text as is.

If you haven't done this on your web page(s) I suggest you do it today. Although META tags are not a secret formula to receiving better placement in search engines, it definitely helps on the engines that use META Tags to index pages. I'll show you some real working examples of effective META tags in the next section.

TIP: Depending on which engine you register with, you are currently allowed a maximum of 1000 or 1024 characters in your keyword META tag. (Where it says "my keywords" in the above example.) Anything beyond that could get your META tag thrown out.

Additional Tips On Placement

A friend and fellow online publisher, Greg Landry, recently did some more research on the particulars of search engine placement and was kind enough to allow me to publish his findings in this book. Some of these tips I've already mentioned but they are important enough to mention again.

The following tips are excerpted from "The Search Engine dilemma ....fact and fiction.... Listing your web site for highest possible placement!":

- When submitting your web site, keep in mind that there are essentially two types of search engines.... "robot" engines that send a "robot" to your site to capture and catalog all the info on your site. These include WebCrawler, Excite, Lycos, Alta Vista, Infoseek, Hotbot, and Inktomi. The second type only uses the info that you give it. These include Yahoo!, WWW Yellow Pages, EINet Galaxy, Open Text, WWW Worm, and World Wide Yellow Pages.

- For best results, always submit your info to each search engine individually rather than using a "submission service". It's important to be able to tailor your info for each specific search engine. It's takes more time but is well worth it!

- Brainstorm for a list of 30 or 40 keywords (or combinations of words like "horse stables") for your site. Then, number the keywords based on what your prospective customer would most likely be using as a keyword. Although you need a strong list of about 20, your first 5 or so will be critical!

- Use the plural when possible. If you list your keyword as "horse stable", but someone searches for "horse stables", it will not find your site. However, if you list your keyword as "horse stables" and someone searches for "horse stable", it will pull up your site!

- The title of your site is **VERY** important! Your title is NOT the first headline on your page, but rather what appears on the title bar of your browser (upper left part of page in Netscape). Most search engines treat the words in your title as MAJOR keywords.....

- Carefully choose two or three keywords to put in your title, but keep in mind that it should not just be a list of keywords....it should make sense. Also, if you make it too long, it will be cut-off. The search engines weigh the importance of a word in your title based on density. For example, if you have five words in your title and one of them is horse, then it will comprise 20% of your title. But, if you only have two words in your title and one of them is horse, then it comprises 50% of your title and is "weighed" much more heavily as a keyword!

- Use your keywords FREQUENTLY in your text at the VERY BEGINNING of your web site. Try not to put tables, graphics or anything else at the top of your site. It should just be text that is rich with your major keywords. Here again, just as in the title, the search engines look at the DENSITY of your keywords rather just the number of keywords. Also, keep in mind that you're NOT just listing keywords here. This is actually the text of your web site.

- "Meta tags" are NOT a magic formula for getting listed at the top of search engines, but they may help on Alta Vista, Hotbot, and Infoseek. A meta tag, for our purposes, is a way of providing a description and keywords that are only visible to the robots from the search engines. However, there is debate over how much weight these are given. The meta tags must go *inside* the header tags, so it looks like this... (see examples on pages 109 and 110.)

- DON'T "keyword spam"! This has been a practice that many have used for good search engine placement....but it's considered bad netiquette and the search engines are all starting to penalize you when they catch it! It's done by repeating keywords *numerous* times either in the meta tag or within the text of the page, sometimes where it can't be seen unless you go to the HTML. I think this is a waste of time now.....and will eventually backfire on you. Just try to legitimately use your keywords as much as you can in the initial paragraphs of text on your web site.

- Be sure that your site is COMPLETELY ready and online before you list your site with any search engines!
- Your title beginning with a letter that's low in the alphabet(abcd) may help in some of the standard search engines such as Yahoo!, but it's really hard to tell how much that comes into play. I certainly would NOT change my site title to something like "AAA horses" just for the sake of starting with an a. If you can legitimately start your title with a,b,c,d, etc., great, otherwise don't worry about it.
- If you're marketing online, many people believe that OVER 50% of your hits will come from Yahoo! It's probably worth spending a considerable amount of your time trying to get good placement on this search engine!
- Be patient......many search engines take weeks to get you in the system.

Here are details on search engines and directories:

YAHOO.....
Technically, Yahoo is not a search engine because it will not visit your web page. Its information on your site is derived from the data you submit. Each submission is reviewed by a "real human".

Yahoo ranks a keyword search based on these criteria...
1. Yahoo categories containing the keyword
2. sites with the keyword in their title
3. sites with the keyword in their description
Limit your description to *10* words!

ALTA VISTA.....
Keyword searches are based on these criteria...
1. Keywords are in the title or in the first few words of your web page.
2. Keywords are close to one another in your page.
3. Keywords are used more than once in your page.
Capitalize any keywords that the searcher may capitalize when searching for your site.

EXCITE.....
Searches favor sites with keywords in the title and then in the text of the site. It also favors keywords that are contained in complete sentences.

HOTBOT.....
Pages with keywords in the title and then in the text are given preference. Hotbot also uses meta tags.

INFOSEEK.....
Pages with keywords at the beginning of the page or in the title do well. Pages with a high frequency of keywords in the text of the page also tend to rank higher.

LYCOS.....

Gives priority to pages with keywords in the title and early in the text of your site.

WEBCRAWLER.....
Pages that match all keywords are listed first and then those that match any keywords. Within these groups, pages with more frequent use of keywords within a page are listed first. It also uses the "concentration" of keywords within a page.

NOTE: All search engines now say that they penalize for "Word spamming" on web sites.....that is just listing keywords numerous times back to back simply to try to "deceive" the search engines.

Greg Landry, M.S. publishes "Successful Online Marketing". This is an excellent, weekly online newsletter. For a free subscription, email Greg@Landry.com

DRIVING MORE TRAFFIC TO YOUR SITE - THE GENUINE "ARTICLE"

Fact: Most small business web sites never see more than a few hundred visitors per week, especially in the first few months of existence. At most of these sites, growth stops at that level. Unfortunately, you just can't generate a lot of income with these numbers.

So how can you start the momentum and keep it growing? Build a funnel to your site!

On only the second month of my web site's existence, my traffic was up to 8,000 hits per month. Not a big deal to many larger web sites, but to a brand new site, not bad. Keep in mind, I had zero banners, a very limited budget and many of my search engine submissions did not kick in for six to eight weeks. At a rate that is growing by more than 75 percent each month, my site will surpass my lofty first year goals without a problem.

So how did I do it?

Well, along with my email newsletter and all of the different methods I have mentioned so far in this book, I utilized a little Yankee ingenuity.

I carry three internet service accounts. That is to say, I have three separate ISP's. My main reason for doing this is insurance. Since I need to get my gazette out every Friday without fail, I figured why rely on one carrier when internet access is so inexpensive. (I pay $19.95 for unlimited access on each account.)

Now, since all of these accounts come with a few megabytes of storage for web hosting, I figured hey, why not use it, right? After all, it doesn't cost any less if I don't.

That's when I decided to build a series of web pages designed to drive traffic to my site. Since I had many internet marketing related articles in the works and many more posted at my web site, I decided that these would make excellent stand alone web pages. And since they were hosted on different domains than my main site, I could get some more play with the search engines. The results were phenomenal.

The articles themselves were already very keyword rich and squeezing in a few more keywords where it was pertinent would not hurt my cause either. Beware: There is a fine line between what search engines consider "the natural occurrence" of keywords and keyword "stuffing" or "spamming." If your document is a good read that happens to be keyword rich, you stand a much better chance at having it appear on a search engine than if is an obvious attempt at deceit.

TIP: If you purposely misspell a few of your keywords, that's actually a good thing. After all, many people searching the web often misspell the words they are searching on. This can work to your advantage.

I was also very careful to name these pages tactfully. Here's an example of a few of my page titles:

Advertising in ezines - Ezine advertising that works!

Direct Email Marketing. Using direct email to sell.

Notice a few important components. Once again the alphabetically-strategic first word, the most important words repeated twice (another helpful tactic), and the interesting nature of the titles themselves. Even the word ezine is mentioned in singular as well as plural in that first title. I *always* employ ALL of these features. They add up to better placement.

The next thing I did as I built my series of article web pages was to place a banner ad to my home page on every article. Readers who happened upon the page and wanted more information about the topic they were researching, could simply click to my main site. Starting to get the picture? Every week I would build a few more pages and register them with all the major search engines. Different keyword rich pages, different domains and all linked to my main site home page.

There is absolutely nothing wrong with using a little creativity when it comes to marketing and promotion. Gather your resources (mine happened to be an abundance of web hosting space and the ability to create web pages) and devise a plan. More than likely, you too can create a "funnel" to your home page in a similar fashion.

Note: If you're looking for a secondary ISP, you can access a list of more than 5,000 worldwide by visiting **http://thelist.iworld.com/** and searching by name or your geographic location.

In addition to creating your own funnel, consider hopping on the bandwagon of a few other netrepreneurs who have achieved visibility. Search your keywords from **http://www.bizweb2000.com/engines.htm** and you will no doubt come across plenty of pages that market the same stuff you are marketing. Consider trading banner links and offer whatever you have to offer to get a link on their site.

If you're wondering how the heck they managed to get ranked so high at a particular search engine, investigate. Look at their html. Once you get to their page, it's as simple as clicking on "view" and "source" in your browser. If this doesn't work, try right clicking on the page (away from images) then left click "view source."

What are they using for META tags? What's their title? How about those keywords? There is absolutely nothing wrong with a little investigative research. I am NOT suggesting you steal their code. What I am suggesting is possibly "modeling" your site after a site that works. There's certainly nothing wrong with that. After all, I've heard that duplication is the highest form of flattery. (Or something like that.) This is also an excellent way to stay abreast of what is working and what is not.

If you prefer, you can model your html after one of my pages. Feel free to replace the description, keywords and title with your own, in the actual html of my high ranking pages. Here are two examples:

Example 1:

```
<html>
<head>
<meta name="description"
content="Access to powerful internet marketing
secrets and strategies. Direct Email Marketing
WITHOUT THE RISK..!">
<meta name="keywords"
content="free help, online marketing, internet
marketing, selling on-line, ezines, home based
```

```
business opportunities, marketing, classified
ads, advertising, income opportunity, making
money, domain name registration, direct email,">
<title>Free Online Marketing Help!</title>
<title>Direct email Marketing !</title>
</head>
```

Check out that code carefully. Notice the alphabetically strong description, descriptive keywords and title, which is actually two titles. (This was a tactic that worked well at a few search engines at the time I posted this page. I learned this by checking out other high ranking pages!) Notice the *repeated* keywords. Don't get carried away or you may get penalized. Seven occurrences of any keyword should be your limit.

Example 2:

```
<html>
<head>
<meta name="description"
content="Autoresponders at discount!">
<meta name="keywords"
content="autoresponders, autoresponder,
AUTORESPONDERS, Autoresponders, auto-responders,
infobot, mailbot, mailbots, online marketing,
internet marketing, selling on-line">
<title>Autoresponders at Discount!</title>
</head>
```

Notice once again the alphabetically strong description, descriptive keywords and title. This code also uses the density factor. That is, my main keyword - autoresponders - makes up thirty-three percent of the description and title tags. Notice again, the repeated keywords and the capitalized and plural versions of each.

In addition to the strategically composed header tags in both of these examples, the content/text of these "articles" were *extremely* keyword rich as well. Don't forget this important component

So there you go, two living working examples of the stuff that works! The pages with the code above were ranked in the top five of five different high profile search engines!

TIP: Here's a service that can help you track your progress in search engine positioning. You can try it for free and for a nominal fee they will provide you with a graph of how your rankings change with time.
http://www.positionagent.com

A few last words on search engine positioning:

You've utilized all the methods suggested here and you've seen your standings improve considerably in the search engines, but you still can't get on that first page of results! Why??

Remember: search engines index literally *millions* of web pages. The more competition you have in your field, the harder it will be for you to get great positioning. (I know this since I've got some stiff competition in the internet marketing arena.)

The more sites competing for space on a search engine, the harder it is to get one of your pages near the top. That's not to say it can't be done. As I mentioned earlier, I have enjoyed quite a long run at several of the most popular search engines by utilizing ALL of the tools I have brought before you in this book.

The important thing to remember is that your web site promotional efforts do not stop with the search engines. Also remember, search engines will not function in their current state forever. (Not to worry, I'll write a new book to keep you abreast of the changes.)

For these reasons and many more you should be using most if not ALL of the tools, techniques and strategies as possible to promote your site. Web site promotion is an ongoing and continuous task. Go forth and use this knowledge wisely!

PARTING WORDS OF WISDOM

KEEP AN EYE OUT

Before you put this book down I have a few parting words of wisdom I'd like to pass on.

First, a few words on diversity. It is a fact that finding new and innovative opportunities in business plays a major role in success. The internet is prime ground for simple and effective diversification. With the power of the computer and the World Wide Web backing you, it is now possible to be involved in many business ventures simultaneously. What's the advantage of doing this? Simple, increased income.

Unlike the real world, internet diversity can take up a very small amount of your time. And here's the best part - in cyberspace, the extra income derived from ancillary projects can result in some handsome profits. Actually, if you chose the right opportunities as they come along, it can result in a windfall of profits!

Cyberspace is a proving ground for entrepreneurs. Every day new businesses are started on the internet. The billions of dollars that have already been made online will surely be dwarfed by the staggering amounts of money that are made over the next few years and beyond.

Absolutely anyone can take advantage of this fact by employing new opportunities. Here are a few do's and don'ts on selecting new business opportunities:

1. DO NOT invest a lot of money into a project that is not your own. Yes, just like in the real world there are

charlatans that will separate you from your hard-earned cash. Look for opportunities with low start up costs.

2. DO NOT spread yourself too thin. Although it's easy to get involved in 20 different ventures online, it's not a good idea. Not only is it impossible to give enough time to properly market each venture, you lose a bit of credibility when you are involved in too many ventures at once.

3. DO pay close attention to new network marketing opportunities. Although I was never a fan of MLM in the real world, cyberspace has changed the face of network marketing forever. Oh sure, there are still *bad* MLM's in cyberspace, but the success of the good ones has been nothing short of phenomenal. The raw number of marketers online combined with cutting edge technology is already writing a new chapter in network marketing.

Already, some very ordinary people have become wealthy through network marketing in cyberspace. (And many more surely will.) This is because it is very easy to duplicate your efforts online. Remember though, it's easy to spread yourself too thin, but don't. In just more than a year online I have diversified my business by joining just two network marketing companies. Both offered free or low-cost start up, excellent products/services and free marketing tools.

KEEP YOUR EYES OPEN! The first chapter of many success stories will be written over the next year or two. Entrepreneurs who are first to the scene will profit the most. That has always been a fact in business and it remains true in the online arena.

Not a day goes by that I don't stop and think about the incredible technological advances that I have been lucky enough to witness. The birth of the internet and it's subsequent rise in popularity through the late 1990s is truly a marvel that I do not take lightly.

Rest assured, the changes at hand will also be nothing short of spectacular. After all, the internet is still in its infancy.

There is no doubt that many lives will be changed in the next year and into the next century. Mine will be one of them. My life has *already* been transformed in a way I never thought possible.

In early 1996, I reached out and grabbed a firm hold on this technological marvel. As the internet has hurled me speeding into the future, I have left behind the shackles of a nine-to-five job, a two-hour commute and a limited career in management. I have never looked back.

I only hope that the knowledge I've shared in this publication allows a great deal of others to do the same.

There is no greater feeling than realizing you *can* control your own destiny. With a little help from the internet, more and more people are beginning to do just that.

Welcome to the future!

HELP WANTED:

A note from the publisher:

I would like to start sending you monthly checks... "Insider Internet Marketing" is already showing incredible sales figures. There is such a demand for this book that I would like to invite you to spread the word. And I'll pay you handsomely for it.

That's right - you can start making money right away! This is a chance to make a substantial income with almost ZERO effort on your part. It's so simple, you may be a bit skeptical. More than a few people have already asked, "Why would you do this?"

Simple. There is just no way I can single-handedly reach the millions of netizens who need this book. By letting people like you spread the word, I'll reach more people than I could reach alone.

"Insider Internet Marketing" can add some big numbers to your online income right away. We are already processing a staggering number of orders daily, why not let us start sending YOU checks too! It takes only a few minutes to sign up. This book will be a hot seller for years. Sign up today at:

http://www.bizweb2000.com/hlpwantd.htm

We'll provide you with all the tools you need, including your own secure deal-closing web site. Don't pass up this opportunity to jump-start your online business!

Sincerely, Jim Daniels
CEO/President - JDD Publishing